Date

D0801934

Oakton Community College
Morton Grove, Illinois

Filmguide to

The General

INDIANA UNIVERSITY PRESS FILMGUIDE SERIES
Harry Geduld and Ronald Gottesman,
General Editors

Filmguide to

The General

E. RUBINSTEIN

INDIANA UNIVERSITY PRESS
Bloomington   London

Published in Canada by Fitzhenry & Whiteside Limited, Don Mills, Ontario
Library of Congress catalog card number: 72–88637
ISBN: 0–253–39309–4 cl.   0–253–39310–8 pa.
Manufactured in the United States of America

contents

preface

FOR JULIET WALLER

My thanks go to Raymond Rohauer, without whose efforts much of Buster Keaton's work would be a subject not of criticism but of speculation; to those who have written on Keaton before me, and especially to Rudi Blesh for his biography; to Charles Affron, Robert Lyons, and Susan Manso for advice and encouragement; to Charles Silver, of the Museum of Modern Art Film Study Center; to Richmond College, CUNY, for student aid funds that allowed me to employ Barbara Robbins as research assistant; to Mrs. Jeanette Cohen of the Richmond College Media Services Department; and because I have no other place to say it, to Buster for all he taught me (and everyone else) about making comedies and making movies.

Filmguide to

The General

credits

THE GENERAL

United Artists Corporation, Buster Keaton Productions, Inc., 1926

Direction	Buster Keaton and Clyde Bruckman
Scenario	Buster Keaton and Clyde Bruckman
Producer	Joseph M. Schenck
Adaptation	Al Boasberg and Charles Smith
Photography	Dev Jennings and Bert Haines
Technical Direction	Fred Gabourie

8 Reels

Premieres: 22 December, 1926, Los Angeles; 7 February, 1927, New York City.

Cast

Annabelle Lee	Marian Mack
Capt. Anderson	Glen Cavender
General Thatcher	Jim Farley
Southern General	Frederick Vroom
Annabelle's Father	Charles Smith
Annabelle's Brother	Frank Barnes
Union Generals	Joe Keaton
	Mike Denlin
	Tom Nawm
Johnnie Gray	Buster Keaton

1

outline

The General

1. PROLOGUE: JOHNNIE'S DISGRACE

Johnnie and Annabelle. "The Western and Atlantic Flyer speeding into Marietta, Ga., in the Spring of 1861." Johnnie Gray, engineer. Train stops. The boys. "There were two loves in his life": his engine, The General; and Annabelle Lee, in photo. Procession to Annabelle's house. Recognition on porch.

Inside. He sits with Annabelle. Tricks boys out of house. Photo of him and The General. Her brother: "Fort Sumter has been fired upon." Brother and father leave to enlist. "Aren't you going to enlist?" Her kiss. His gestures and fall.

Recruiting Office. Johnnie first in line. Rejected ("He is more valuable to the South as an engineer.") Measures himself against others. "William Brown. Bartender." Steals acceptance paper. Kicked out. "If you lose this war don't blame me."

Annabelle's father and brother outside. Johnnie turns away. *Annabelle's Scorn.* Johnnie in front of The General. Sits on cross bar.

In Annabelle's house: "He's a disgrace to the South."

Annabelle at The General: "I don't want you to speak to me again until you are in uniform"; exit.

In Annabelle's house: father sorts papers, throws out photo. Johnnie on driving bar. Train starts.

2. THE FIRST CHASE

The Plan. "A year later. In a Union encampment just north of Chattanooga." General Thatcher and Captain Anderson plot to steal the W. & A. train at Big Shanty, burn bridges along Southern army's route.

Marietta: Annabelle with brother. She boards train to visit injured father.

"Big Shanty—twenty minutes for dinner." Spies take engine and baggage cars; Annabelle trapped. Johnnie washing hands. Sees The General moving; runs. Telegraph wires cut.

Johnnie Pursues. Handcar. Bicycle. Reaches Southern camp, gets train and troops. Troop car not engaged to engine (The Texas). Johnnie hooks on cannon. Spies on The General see The Texas. Chase. Johnnie and water tower. Johnnie and cannon. Spies detach first car. Spies toss logs onto track. Spies throw switch. The Texas reverses, is stuck; Johnnie throws dirt. Burning car. Southern armies retreat, Northern advance. He chops. Broken axe. Sees troops. Spies throw logs from trestle. Johnnie jumps off. Top hat and tree. Alone in forest. Storm.

3. JOHNNIE RESCUES ANNABELLE

At Union Headquarters. Johnnie at window. Enters. Steals food. Hides under table. The meeting of Union generals. Sneeze, pounding, boots, cigar burn. Annabelle brought in, is locked in bedroom. Meeting breaks up.

Escape. Johnnie crawls out. The two sentries. Annabelle's room, her awakening. Out the window. Lightning. Bear. Animal trap. "We had better stay here till daybreak to see where we are." Annabelle's gratitude.

Morning. Northern camp. Johnnie sees The General. The shoes. Annabelle in sack. She unpins The General plus baggage car. Is deposited with other baggage. Johnnie takes The General.

4. THE SECOND CHASE

The General Pursued. Johnnie pulls down telegraph pole. Pole on tracks. He rescues Annabelle. Stop for firewood. Annabelle's trap. Union soldiers lashed to engine. Rear wall of baggage car, barrels, cases on tracks. Water tower. Annabelle sweeps. Annabelle stokes. The Texas hooks on; Johnnie disengages baggage car. Throws switch, bends rail. Annabelle drives, Johnnie on hill. The General reverses. Union soldiers on unfinished inclined track, rolls back. Northerners and bent rail.
Rock River Bridge. Johnnie builds fire. Trapped. Leaps—into river. Back on The General. Southern soldier shoots, Johnnie puts on gray uniform.

5. THE BATTLE

The Return. Southern general; Johnnie explains Union advance. Alarm. Troops move. General mounts. Johnnie and Annabelle amid the charge. Annabelle's father. Johnnie alone in street. Sword; he falls.
The Other Side. Union train. Rail fixed by axe. Union troops meet train. "That bridge is not burned enough to stop you. . . ." Train on bridge. Collapses. Train in river. Southern troops attack. Union cavalry retreats.
Johnnie the Soldier. Battle scenes. Southern general commands. Johnnie helps. Johnnie's sword and scabbard. Cannoneers and Union sniper. Johnnie mans cannon. Dam bursts. Union troops retreat. Johnnie seizes flag.
"Heroes of the Day." Johnnie marches with cavalry. Reunited with The General, finds Thatcher aboard, leads him to Confederate general. Johnnie stripped of uniform. "Enlist the lieutenant." "Occupation?" "Soldier." With Annabelle on cross bar. Soldiers, saluting.

the creator:

Buster Keaton

In one dressing room, but each at his own table, two men work at transforming the natural terrors of their aged faces into the artificial sadness of comic masks. Soon we see them together on stage: one is to play the violin, the other to accompany at the piano. But the pianist's score pours in a steady flow from its stand, and the fiddler's leg keeps retreating alarmingly into the immense expanse of his trousers, and tuning the violin develops into a project so complex that it finally necessitates removing all the strings from the piano (which nonetheless sounds just fine), and the pianist finds himself wearing a crushed fiddle like a bizarre snowshoe on his right foot, and the violinist falls to pieces at the unbearable sweetness of his own music, and at last, in a frenzy of allegro, the accompanist is ejected from his bench, still clawing maniacally in the direction of the keyboard, while his partner fiddles himself straight into the pit and is returned to the stage enthroned in a mutilated bass drum. The act is over. The audience goes wild. Then, backstage, as the pianist looks on, the fiddler dies.

What I've been attempting to describe is the climactic episode of Chaplin's *Limelight* (1952). For the only time in their long careers, the two most wonderful of the mute actor-comedians are performing together: it's Charlie on the violin, Buster Keaton at the piano. Each, in the presence of the other, recaptures the full force of his unique style: Chaplin, as always, gets

5

caught up in himself—in the mysterious spaces of his own pants, in the beauty of the music only he knows how to make, ultimately in his very passion for his own performance; Keaton, his eyes as devastating as ever behind inch-thick prop spectacles, doggedly struggles to make it through an operation in which almost every object in sight slyly turns on him. Together they share the last fully realized, lunatic, liberating slapstick turn either would execute before a camera.

But as my summary indicates, this high point of the history of screen comedy takes place in a larger dramatic scheme: Calvero, the clown—Chaplin, of course—after years of neglect and poverty, for one triumphant moment regains his audience; and then, watching from the wings as his protégée, a young dancer, succeeds him in public adulation, he very quietly but very conspicuously expires. The glory of his onstage performance is thus seen in a context at once profoundly bitter and wildly self-indulgent—a context definitively Chaplinesque.

And there exists a still larger context in which we must locate our response to the slapstick concert: I mean in the lives of Chaplin and Keaton themselves. If *Limelight* is Chaplin's supreme (and, I think, sublime) expression of self-pity and his most acrid statement of what it means to watch the world turn its back, it is nonetheless precisely an "expression" and a "statement"—it is the movie that he wanted to make and therefore made; with enough of a public left to justify, at least to himself, the production and release of *Limelight,* Chaplin stages his own demise in full view, and in tacit defiance, of the audience whose obdurate fickleness he is in the process of demonstrating. Keaton, on the other hand, in happier days Chaplin's only serious rival in the arts of screen comedy, appears for his turn—at Chaplin's bidding in life, at Calvero's in the film—does his job, is admitted to the group of those privileged to stand about as the great man dies, and then presumably returns to the actual shadows, the palpable oblivion from which he has briefly emerged. The lessons Chaplin seeks to teach are therefore, paradoxically, far more pertinent to Keaton's unhappy career than to his own; whether or not Chaplin himself missed this final irony of *Limelight,* Buster Keaton, I suspect, with twenty years of public indifference already behind him, did not.

BEGINNINGS

The story that leads from the variety stage to Fatty Arbuckle to *The Boat* to *The General* to *Limelight* to *How to Stuff a Wild Bikini* begins on October 4, 1895, in Piqua, Kansas with the birth of Joseph Frank Keaton. His parents, Joe and Myra, are performers in a traveling medicine show, later vaudevillians, and their child's world is boarding houses and theater wings. At the age of six months, he receives his more familiar name from his parents' friend, the legendary escape artist Harry Houdini (some of whose tricks he is later to learn and execute on stage and in film): watching the infant laughing after having bounced down a whole flight of stairs, Houdini compliments him on his splendid "buster." The name by which Keaton is ever after to be known is thus the first testimony to that physical indomitability which marks, from the beginning, one of the two most obvious qualities of his performing style; the second, already adumbrated by 1898 when he pressures his parents into allowing him to make an appearance in the family act, is of course what is known, not at all accurately, as the Keaton deadpan, the hypnotic mien of solemn and imperturbable concentration.

By the end of 1901, a new act, The Three Keatons, is exposed to the audiences of the Wonderland Theatre in Wilmington, Delaware. The essence of the act is like nothing they have seen: a small child, making a chaos of his father's life by his obsessive pursuit of imaginary flies, is in turn hurled and swatted across the stage, against backdrops, into the wings, as if death and dismemberment were not to be entertained as possible consequences. The pattern of Buster's success is set: wherever he appears—and the Gerry Society, whose mission it is to tend to the enforcement of the recent laws governing the employment and exploitation of children, does what it can to see that he appears as infrequently as possible—Buster causes a sensation. His art develops: the falls become ever more startling and perilous, while Buster's face—whether in recognition of the dangers at hand, or of the comic effects of his refusal to smile, or, as seems likely, of both at once—fixes into ever-greater seriousness and intentness. But "art" may be a misleading term when applied to those vaudeville days, at least to the degree that it fails to hint at the essentially improvisatory quality of the Keatons' work, fails to suggest the delight taken by two natural athlete-comedians in testing, before an audience, the limits of each other's skill and endurance. Rudi Blesh, Keaton's official biographer, summarizes neatly: "Joe and Buster would ring a thousand changes in the act for seventeen years, but from beginning to end it would remain in essence what it had always been—the same old romp that had begun in a Kansas boardinghouse between a father and his two-year-old son."[1]

Until 1915, The Three Keatons flourish. But over the next two years, Joe's encounters with temper, temperament, and alcohol finally demolish the act. Buster promptly receives an offer of a solo turn in the Shubert brothers' Broadway revue, *The Passing Show of 1917*. But this potentially prestigious debut in musical comedy is never realized. Shortly after receiving the Shuberts' offer, he visits the Schenck Studios in New York, where Roscoe "Fatty" Arbuckle and his troupe are filming one of their comedies. Overwhelmed by the technical and comic possibilities of movie-making, he accepts Arbuckle's on-the-spot invitation to become a member of the company and immediately goes to work. Keaton's extraordinary affinity for his new medium is evident even in *The Butcher Boy* (1917), the first of his fourteen or fifteen[2] two-reel comedies for Arbuckle. Fatty is of course the star and center of the action—or rather the actions, for, like many Arbuckle comedies, the picture splits into a pair of autonomous one-reel narratives, quite mysterious in their connection. In the second half, except for some spectacular falls, Keaton is barely evident; it would be difficult, I suppose, for any performer to stand out against the grotesque, disquieting, sometimes even amusing spectacle of Fatty in Mary Pickford drag. But in the first half, Arbuckle, whose generosity Keaton will always acknowledge with gratitude and affection, allows his debut player to take over for a few minutes. What occurs is astonishing.

Keaton's entrance in *The Butcher Boy* is comparable to nothing else I know in the history of movies. What we see is not some gifted player tentatively assaying his relation to the space around him, nor some player trained in another medium attempting to substitute a foreign style, however impressive, for an essentially cinematic manner; we are privileged to observe an uncanny moment of self-realization on the part of a man of twenty-one who, after a lifetime of training in vaudeville, has discovered his natural metier. The comedy takes place in a general store. Fatty himself plays the butcher, and he has had ample occasion to display his skills: he has lobbed hunks of meat casually onto awaiting hooks with the precision of basketball virtuosi; over his shoulder he has tossed knives which, after a more than respectable number of turns, have landed point down and embedded themselves in the butcher block behind him; he has rolled a cigarette in one hand with a facility that can only give one pause. He has done his job so well that, had Keaton and Chaplin never existed, he might well seem a supreme exemplar of pantomimic accomplishment. But then comes Buster.

"This first film appearance of Keaton's is worth detailing at length," says David Robinson, "for it gives us some idea of the equipment he brought from vaudeville to the cinema. It shows him already, in his first day's work in pictures, imposing his own rhythm, his own sense of timing and construction of a gag upon a team given to much less disciplined modes of comedy creation."[3] We notice at once the economy of Keaton's gestures, the patience with which a gag premise is followed to its inescapable conclusion. And we also notice, from the very instant of his arrival, the extraordinary intensity with which he assays his position in a world of objects. The moment he appears, in hayseed costume plus vaudeville slapshoes and the soon-to-be-legendary flat hat, he proceeds to pluck bristles from some brooms massed in an urn near the door; satisfied with his assessment of the brooms, and having accidentally stepped into the drippings of a vat of molasses, with his finger he wipes the bottom of his shoe, and later the spout itself, for a careful taste. Buster enters this small scene as he will enter thousands more in the course of the next decade: examining, testing, evaluating. But even cautious, prudent experimentation, he learns, is no match for chance, fate, and the things of this world. Into the can he's carrying he drops a coin to pay for some molasses. Fatty fills the can. The coin is now irretrievable. While Buster turns away, Fatty empties the can into Buster's hat, then returns the molasses to the can. Buster puts on his hat, which of course becomes firmly fixed to his head. As he tries to remove it, he drops the can: his feet become just as firmly trapped in a new pool of molasses on the floor. By now the molasses, which he has so recently tested and judged, has asserted its malevolent ascendancy. Fatty tries everything, including boiling water, to free his customer. Gradually we realize that Fatty doesn't want merely to liberate him, but rather to get him out of the store at any cost. This he finally accomplishes by means of a violent kick: up goes Buster, across the store, down a short flight of stairs onto his skull, then head over heels on the sidewalk. So much for buying a can of molasses.

But it isn't long before he's back for more. This time he finds himself in the midst of a fight between Arbuckle and Al St. John in which sacks of flour are the chosen weapon. Buster is at once pelted, of course, and joins the melee; we soon have the sense that a snowstorm has somehow made its way into the store, for the air itself is largely flour. Before it is over, however, the scene becomes Buster's once again. The camera pulls back: the balcony of the store, heretofore unimportant save as the place where the pretty ingénue sits to blink and smile, is now made to appear a challenging part of the cinematic space Buster must subdue. As usual when Keaton's energies are released, the ostensible functions of the physical components of any scene are subject to review: poles, for example, do not merely hold up balconies, they are there to be climbed; and so, in a moment, Buster has mastered vertical space as well as horizontal and our focus is now on his movements on the higher level. Like nobody else before or since, Buster Keaton shows that the term "scene-stealing" can possess an almost literal sense.

Seen beside the Keaton two-reelers to come, let alone the great feature-length comedies of 1923 to 1928, *The Butcher Boy* is minor stuff: the imagination behind it is, after all is said and done, not Keaton's but Arbuckle's. Yet those basic assumptions that will guide Buster's movements through the great years of his screen career are already operative, already a natural and recognizable part of his performing style. First, there's the complexity of his response to Things: we see it here in the hint of that scrupulous initial attention he will always pay to new objects, large and small, an attention based in part on the recognition that, as demonstrated by the apparently guileless molasses that proves to be an agency of entrapment, no one living in a world of Things can be too careful; we'll see it again and again, most memorably perhaps in his response to the series of machines—i. e., Things with moving parts, all the more crafty and unpredictable than their simpler brothers—which are at once Keaton's particular delight and Keaton's characteristic foes, and which, by the time of *The Navigator* and *The General,* are exalted to the status of co-stars. Second, there's the physical freedom, a combination of resilience (since life means getting knocked on your head, better learn to stand up again) and daring (make the environment yours before the environment makes you its). Both these traits are as adaptable to Arbuckle's genre of screen comedy as to The Three Keatons' vaudeville turns: no wonder Keaton at once finds a place in the Arbuckle troupe; no wonder that his movie debut takes place, as he will proudly recall, without benefit of a single retake[4]; no wonder that, within two years, he'll have learned all that Arbuckle has to teach about the production of screen comedy and will set out on his own.

KEATON IN CHARGE

By the beginning of 1920, the producer Joseph Schenck is ready to reopen the former Chaplin studios under Keaton's name; there, with only a few weeks off to star in a Metro feature called *The Saphead,* Keaton makes no less than nineteen two-reel shorts over three years. His working conditions are, and will remain until 1928, very nearly ideal: he has his own studio and his own staff, and he can boast grosses so impressive that nobody tries very hard to interfere with his operations. The great days of his creativity have begun.

With his two-reelers, Keaton is free to explore the particularities of his comic temperament. (1) His responses to the challenges of the physical world become ever more canny and ever more daring: I think first of the conquest of the monstrous steamboat paddle wheel in *Day Dreams,* and of the incredible four-person human pyramid (originally designed as an elopement machine for second-storey brides) lurching along the streets in *Neighbors,* and of the ladder-bridge across an actual ravine that Buster must construct for himself, rung by rung, even as he crosses it, in *The Paleface.* (2) Conversely, the gag props become ever more elaborate and ever more perilous, culminating perhaps in *The Electric House* where, as the portentous title implies, the entire physical environment looks quietly forward to the undoing of mere human agents. (3) A strange melancholy, bordering on morbidity, makes itself felt, most inescapably in the last scene of *Cops:* Buster, mistaken for a criminal, has just outwitted a small army of police; but then his girl rejects him; whereupon he simply turns back into the station house, and *The End* is seen printed across a tombstone on which sits the flat Keaton hat. (4) Disorienting dream-like images are introduced, sometimes dwelt upon, as in *The Playhouse,* where nearly all the characters, including every last member of a theater orchestra, are played by Keaton; or, in a different vein, in *One Week,* where the assembling of a prefabricated house brings forth upon the earth a monster-building each of whose parts is identifiable and functional but whose overall misshapenness shares something with the vision of the Surrealists.

Perhaps preëminently among the shorts, however, audiences remember, and critics discuss, *The Boat,* an unexceptionable synthesis of all the elements of Keaton's now richly ripened style. The casualness of design of the Arbuckle shorts is gone, replaced by Keaton's distinctive clarity and unity of structure; everything in *The Boat* develops from one simple premise, namely that a man and his family want to go to sea in their home-built vessel. For all the man's amazing mechanical inventiveness, nothing finally goes right: all his possessions—house, car, the boat itself and everything on it—are destroyed or lost, and, at the end, he and his wife and his children, after a miraculous eleventh-hour rescue from death by water, walk off to meet some kind of new existence on some unknown, benighted shore.

Although the major characters manage to survive, *The Boat* must—and should—sound bleak indeed for the report it bears of a man's aspiration to conquer his world; it isn't easy to think of any work of narrative art that encompasses quite so many disasters in quite so short a space. Yet Keaton's resignation carries with it Keaton's resiliency: defeat, though as inevitable as death, unlike death always implies another chance, and human life consists in taking foolish chances. And somehow, for all the nightmare, *The Boat* almost never ceases to be funny, because Keaton's mastery of the visual gag is now as complete as it will ever be. Every reversal is expressed in such irresistibly comic terms that, even as one wonders whether to laugh or to cry, one finds oneself howling through the decision.

Take the most famous scene of all, the first launching of the cursed boat. Buster stands in triumph on the prow. With devastating slowness the boat inches down the incline into the water—and, once there, never for an instant deviates from its solemn downward course, until all that is left to see of boat and skipper is a famous flat hat afloat on an empty sea. Through it all, Buster is seen from the rear. Only once does his face punctuate the ineluctable movement of the boat: at the moment when even he has to admit that the unimaginable is actually taking place, his head jerks momentarily backward; I lack the language to designate all that his clear, fierce eyes are saying. And what makes the scene so unmistakably Keaton's, in addition to, and inseparable from, the gag itself and Keaton's facial expression, is the absolute, imperturbable clarity with which it is seen. Two shots do it, one far and high from behind the boat, the second, only somewhat closer and lower, from the dock to the right of the boat. Such "all-revealing, long-take long shots" are, to borrow David Robinson's decisive words, "as frank in their gaze as Keaton himself."[5] The style of the performer and the style of the director come together. The vision is manifestly, unarguably Keaton's. The apprentice has become the author.

the production— and after

In 1923, Keaton follows Chaplin and Harold Lloyd into the production of feature comedies (meaning, in Keaton's case, films running from five to eight reels). For the next five years, he is to produce two movies annually. Each will cost somewhat under a quarter million dollars and some will gross nearly ten times that figure.[1] The production arrangement remains entirely felicitous: though released at first through Metro and later through United Artists, the films issue from Keaton's own studio and Keaton's own imagination. The fact that he sometimes shares or even entirely gives away official directorial credit should not be taken very seriously, except perhaps as a token of his often reckless generosity: we have Keaton's own word and, still more persuasively, the testimony of our own eyes to assure us that these are indeed Keaton's movies in design and in execution, the natural outgrowth of all that is invaluable and individual in the shorts.

In the realm of acting we now observe one striking development of Keaton's art: the range of his performances is astonishing and unique. Even in the two-reelers, Keaton, unlike any of the other major comic actors of the twenties, does not simply carry one perfected impersonation from film to film. One familiar costume does recur: the slapshoes and what James Agee has called the "deadly horizontal hat, as flat and thin as a phonograph record"[2] and the oversize collar and the pinned-on tie all signify Buster as explicitly as the tramp outfit signifies Charlot;

15

but as the comic tonality of the shorts is highly varied, so too documentably if more subtly is the Keaton performance. But even the shorts scarcely suffice to ready us for the final evolution of Keaton the actor. From the mercurial Johnnie Gray of *The General* to the effete young millionaires of *The Navigator* and *Battling Butler* (and even these, as more than one critic has noticed, are far from identical characterizations), from the scholarly sap of the beginning of *College* to the beautiful dandy of the beginning of *Our Hospitality* or the melancholic Friendless of *Go West,* Keaton's acting is no less various than the periods and locations in which the films are set.

But "acting" may be an inapposite label for what Keaton does, at least to the degree that it denotes that which is usually done by actors: his impersonations, like those of a classic mime or, perhaps more nearly, those of a great dancer, depend less on the weight of specific gestures than on the basic qualities of his bodily placement and movement. In the opening scenes of *Battling Butler,* the tiny tilt of the head with which the grotesquely spoiled millionaire acknowledges his mother or his valet is different in more than mere degree from the forward protraction of the neck as Johnnie Gray peers from his locomotive at an autonomous boxcar that keeps vanishing and reappearing before his eyes; so too is Butler's spine, so taut in its slight arc, very unlike the determined backbone of Johnnie in action. Just as a dancer's subtle devices of characterization derive from, and couldn't exist without, the same physical control that makes possible his bold virtuoso movements, Keaton's acting draws upon that singular command of his body that enables him to perform the most perilous stunts without help from stand-ins or from trick camera work.

Also evident by the time of the second of the features, *Our Hospitality,* is the degree to which Keaton has learned to satisfy his passion for neatness and order and credibility. Compared to the Arbuckle shorts—compared to most silent comedies of any length—most of Keaton's two-reelers are models of unity and coherence; compared to his features their construction sometimes appears casual indeed. For what now counts above all is the unbroken flow of the dramatic line, from the simple given conflict (usually Buster is in love but, for one reason or another, can't have the girl) to the final happy resolution (the result of Buster's myopic determination to win the day). Ideally, no extended episodes or even incidental gags should be permitted to interrupt the progress of the narrative or detract from the dramatic logic of a scene; what is more, those gags that are admitted, however extraordinary the immediate demands they lay upon the hero, must never seem quite impossible or what Keaton often refers to disdainfully as "ridiculous." (If, for example, a scene in *The General* calls persuasively for the presence of a sword, a sword is introduced; given Keaton's sense of Things, it's not likely to lend itself to whatever plans its user has in mind and will therefore serve as the source of any number of maddening misadventures; but its presence is, in the first place, neither gratuitous nor distracting, and any consequent comic business must remain within the province of the plausible.) So it is that a bare plot outline of most of his pictures would seem something other than comedy: they stand as perfect exemplifications of François Mars's theory that a good comic story must be an "action . . . perfectly serious and perfectly sufficient unto itself . . . onto which the gags attach themselves like inopportune parasites."[3]

The General stands as a clear example. Keaton's source is William Pittenger's *The Great Locomotive Chase,* a first-hand narration of one of the most extraordinary adventures of the Civil War: a band of twenty Northern raiders (Pittenger among them), disguised as Southern civilians, purloined a Confederate locomotive near Atlanta and, destroying bridges and telegraph communications along the route, attempted to make their way to Union-occupied Chattanooga. In order for *The Great Locomotive Chase* to become a Keaton movie, however, a few alterations are called for. (1) The entire narrative is shifted to the Confederate point of view, more specifically to that of the one little Southern engineer who single-handedly pursues the kidnappers of his beloved engine. At once the Keatonian possibilities of the narrative are clarified. (2) The Keatonian heroine—she to whom the protagonist must prove himself—is introduced in order to establish, conventionally and therefore simply, the overall dramatic framework in which all the hero's actions are to be located. (In this case she is named—a bit alarmingly, if one stops to consider it—for Poe's Annabelle Lee.) Then, to keep the whole adventure as unified and compact as possible, Keaton contrives that she find herself aboard the stolen train. (3) The hero, at the Union encampment to which his pursuit of his locomotive has taken him, must steal back the train, thus giving rise to a second chase to balance and comment upon the first. Thus countless variants on locomotive gags can be effected while the structure of the film remains unimpeachably symmetrical. (4) For the climactic episode, still another locomotive chase being pretty clearly out of the question, we're given some battle scenes, without specific source in Pittenger's story but hardly an illogical appendage to a narrative set in the Civil War.

The result of all this reworking and reordering of materials is the most classical of movie comedies, a film that amply satisfies in cinematic terms the Renaissance demand for the three Unities—of Time, of Place, and of Action. Following what I call "The Prologue"—in other words, beginning with the title "A year later"—the events of the movie are acted out within twenty-four hours. Place is limited during the main action by the design of railroad tracks—from a town in Georgia to the Union camp and back again. As for Action, especially in the Aristote-

lian implications of that word—that is, not only the scheme of
events but the motives that engender it—the impluse that ani-
mates *The General* could hardly be simpler: "to have my Annabelle and to have my General," distinct but coordinate urges,
manifestly and absolutely direct Johnnie Gray's every movement
and so the plan of the film. Always in his features, Keaton operates in horror of fuzziness and clutter, but nowhere else quite so
fanatically as in *The General*.

(It seems to me worth pausing to consider the what now
seem extraordinary conditions under which all these adjustments
were effected. In the summer of 1926, Clyde Bruckman presented Keaton with a copy of *The Great Locomotive Chase*.
Seizing at once upon its comic possibilities, Keaton went to
work. In intense collaboration not only with Bruckman [his co-
director] and his writers but with cameramen, technical director,
and so on, Keaton first set up the outlines of a story, insisting
only that an acceptable beginning and ending be established before actual production commenced; as always in the days of
Keaton Studios, there was no written script and no shooting
schedule. Whatever was lacking from the rough preliminary scenario—the gags, in effect—was for the most part invented in the
course of the eight weeks or so of shooting—yet it was nearly
always the first take of any given scene that went into the final
print. Keaton himself did all the final cutting and editing.[4] Before the end of the year *The General* as we know it had its pre-
miere. How so elegant a film as *The General* could emerge from
such ostensibly informal procedures seems to me one of the lost
secrets of movie-making.)

Moreover, in *The General* as in all the features, Keaton's attention to detail is as ardent as his insistence on a neat story.
Authentic period locomotives are unearthed in Georgia and re-
conditioned; shooting, on the other hand, must take place in
Oregon where sufficient old narrow-gauge track remains for the

extended chases. The engines must be powered by real steam produced in a real firebox (a decision that results in a real forest fire). The Oregon State Guard is conscripted for the battle scenes. No miniatures are employed: when the moment arrives for one of the locomotives to drop from a burned-out bridge, an actual engine plunges into an actual river; Blesh tells us that "she still lies where she fell, in a river near Cottage Grove, Oregon, still luring tourists to the spot."[5] For Keaton at his best, comedy is a question of not lying about anything.

LATER

In 1928, ignoring the advice of Chaplin and Lloyd, Keaton allows Schenck to persaude him to dissolve his own company and sign his name to a contract with Metro-Goldwyn-Mayer. The results of this move are quick and disastrous. His staff, brought with him from Keaton Studios according to the terms of the contract, is soon scattered throughout the vast MGM operation. He is ordered to work from a written script devised by various Metro "experts." He somehow manages, despite all the interference, to turn out one authentic Keaton film, *The Cameraman.* Then comes *Spite Marriage;* those fortunate enough to have seen it tend to admire it. But finally Keaton is bested by the Metro system and the new exigencies of sound production. His movies (with the exception of *Doughboys,* according to Blesh[6]) are increasingly unimpressive; his audience soon gets the message. His professional nightmare aggravated by personal crises, he begins to drink far too much. After 1933, there are no more Metro features.

He tries a film in France, another, embarrassing to watch, in England, and, back in Hollywood, a slew of cheap, largely wretched features and shorts (some of the latter released under the horrifying label of "Educational Pictures"). By the mid-

1940s he is reduced to occasional appearances in mostly fourth-rate movies, to working up gags for Red Skelton, and to various other meaningless odd jobs. He later appears in night clubs and at state fairs and in European circuses. With the advent of television, first in variety shows and later also in commercials, his face is once again highly visible (and he is once again well paid), but the years of defeat and alcohol have done to him what such years do, and, with the exception of the one divine moment in *Limelight,* he will never again fully reactivate the powers of sorcery that were his in the twenties.

At the same time, the quality of his earlier work is rediscovered. After World War II, especially in England and France, he becomes the darling of film societies, and, in the heyday of existentialism, an idol of the intellectuals. The American film historian Raymond Rohauer leads the campaign to restore to the public—and, financially, to Keaton—many films once thought forever lost. By 1965, the year before his death, the deification is nearly complete. He is the focus of two short *hommages* from Canada, one, *The Railroader,* a nostalgic extended reference to the railroad imagery of *The General* (and, more than incidentally, a visual hymn to the glories of the Canadian National Railway), the other a biographical profile, *Keaton Rides Again.* In the same year, he stars—solo—in a fifteen-minute affair called *Film* written expressly for him by Samuel Beckett himself. But also in the same year, he's obliged to toss off appearances in an Italian opus called *Due Marines e un General* and in three of those notorious American International quickies whose titles say only too much: *Pajama Party, Beach Blanket Bingo, How To Stuff a Wild Bikini.*[7] Amid such ironies the chronicle peters out. But Keaton seldom complains: he has, after all, recognized from the start that experience is built on incongruity, just as his screen incarnation has always known that getting through life is quite taxing enough without having to remember to smile.

analysis

1. THE PROLOGUE

Johnnie and Annabelle. The first irony of *The General,* an irony that directs us to the essence of Keaton's cinema, resides in its title. Just as in *The Navigator* the eponym is not, as one might innocently suppose, the man who controls the ship's direction but the ship itself, so The General is not a he but an it, not a military hero but a locomotive. That the name isn't Keaton's invention—it's taken from William Pittenger's factual account of *The Great Locomotive Chase*—is scarcely to the point: it says what Keaton wanted us to hear so clearly that he conferred the title upon the film as a whole. One primary object of our attention is to be a machine, and for Keaton the machine is, as I've already indicated, only a more complicated manifestation of the Thing: fascinating and multifarious in itself, it inspires in the human who encounters it, whether would-be ally or would-be adversary, a totally unexpected range of courage and invention. And this machine lives up to its name: though kidnapped and rekidnapped in the course of the film, it is able, when it wishes, to exercise its power of making the final decisions and giving the orders—like any good general.

The opening shot is of a train, "The Western and Atlantic Flyer speeding into Marietta, Ga., in the Spring of 1861"; the camera eye first follows its progress from a respectful distance, then moves in to show the punctilious engineer examining and flicking dust from his cab. There is no hint of the trouble and complexity to come. The train is in beautiful service to its driver.

The subsequent shots underscore the sense of control, of fulfilled purpose. The train stops, and Johnnie Gray alights to receive a hero's welcome from a pair of adoring boys, from his assistant engineer, from the crowd descending from the train. Beyond the adoration, the gleaming engine is his; so too, presumably, is the Annabelle Lee whose tintype is affixed to one of The General's walls. The shot of the tintype is echoed by a loving shot of Annabelle in the flesh. All appears perfectly harmonious.

The complications set in as Johnnie leads the march to Annabelle's house. The procession, always seen in its totality, consists of Johnnie, then one of the boys, then, at the same distance, the other boy. Slowly the relation of this scene to the opening shot asserts itself: the procession is clearly a visual reminiscence of a train, and the viewer can begin to sense the force of Keaton's controlling metaphor. Johnnie takes off his hat as he passes various townspeople; so, in loving admiration, does the first boy; the second, who has no hat, makes a stab at the same gesture, but empty-handed. The scene assumes an oddly mechanical, nonhuman dimension, and the effect is intensified by the set, unsmiling faces of the participants. And then Annabelle, whom the procession passes by as she stands in a neighbor's yard, falls into place behind the second boy. Though there is no suggestion that Annabelle is motivated by malice, her action results in the transformation of Johnnie the hero into Johnnie the fool of fate: the object of his pilgrimage has been hooked onto the rear of his own train. We see a man proceeding carefully and conscientiously toward a goal he drags behind him. We have entered in earnest the world of Buster Keaton.

The procession has attained Annabelle's porch before Johnnie's awareness catches up with that of the audience. As he buffs his boots on his trousers and knocks, Annabelle has already entered the frame—indeed, standing closer to the camera than the others, she dominates it, thereby underscoring the absurdity of

Johnnie's misunderstanding. When at last he sees her, the great Keaton eyes fix in a great Keaton stare. But here, as always, the inscrutable is best left alone. Annabelle is on the porch. So be it. They enter the house.

Once inside, Johnnie sits down with Annabelle on a sofa. The two boys sit on another; they are obviously going to be in the way. Consciously manipulating their mechanized response to his every gesture, Johnnie rises and puts on his hat. They do the same—at least the one equipped with a hat does. Johnnie opens the door. They file out. Johnnie closes the door, removes his hat, and sits down again beside Annabelle. The episode takes only a few seconds, yet it is unforgettable for the absolute calm and absolute clarity of gesture with which Johnnie attains his objective. This is the other side of the Keaton coin, the requisite complement of the unfortunate procession just concluded; this is Johnnie in control of things—in control of Things. Seen together, these two sequences embody the pattern of the film, the movement from reversal to mastery, from momentary confusion to momentary sway.

What follows this small but flawless triumph is a moment of complete harmony, the last until the final frames of the movie. The elements are simple: Johnnie and Annabelle and The General are together. And so, as Johnnie presents Annabelle with a photo, which Annabelle lovingly props upright on the table, it is an image not only of himself but of himself in front of his engine. The identity of Johnnie's two obsessive attachments will be touched on again and again, but here it receives its simplest visual statement.

By now all that is lacking is a cause in the name of which the intensity of the attachments can be tested and proven; it is provided with the directness and economy so characteristic of Keaton's narrative style. He cuts to Annabelle's father in his room, looking edgily out the window; then back to the parlor, the father opening the door of his room at the left of the screen as Annabelle's brother enters from outside on the right. This image of nervous activity contrasts ominously with the placidity of Johnnie and Annabelle, their heads seen in the foreground from the rear over the back of the sofa. "Fort Sumter has been fired upon," announces the brother; "Then the war is here," replies the father; "Yes, dad, and I'm going to be one of the first to enlist." After their exit, Annabelle, her little plump face now oddly affecting, asks Johnnie, "Aren't you going to enlist too?" He recognizes his obligation. At the door, boldly, she kisses him. Inspired to we cannot imagine what acts of daring to match the daring of her kiss, he flies out the door.

End of the scene. Or not quite the end, for Keaton can seldom resist the final gag, the conclusive ironic statement, here characteristically delivered in a single shot. On the porch, Johnnie faces Annabelle and strikes a wildly romantic attitude—one hand on his heart, the other pointing upward in token of love and aspiration. Whereupon he falls smack off the porch. Whereupon he springs up and resumes the pose before dashing off. Johnnie's little coda is our first hint of Keaton's unexampled physical resilience, of which we are to see so many astonishing illustrations. But it is more: in its admixture of absurdity and purity of intention, it provides a comment on the ethical significance of the simple-minded titles about the coming of the Civil War quoted in the preceding paragraph. The Confederacy in *The General* is in no sense a rational cause. Not a hint is given of the premises of the war. No black face is ever glimpsed. For Keaton the Confederacy is only a perfect metaphor of a gratuitous gallantry, of a devotion all the more absurd and no less comprehensible for being spent in a cause we know is doomed from the outset. In shifting the focus of Pittenger's narrative from the North to the South, Keaton gave full scope to his ironic sense of human aspiration. The Confederacy of *The General* is a preposterous, thus definitively human gesture, struck too close to the edge of a plain, real porch.

Recruiting Office. This sequence might at first appear to be just expository. Johnnie has to be rejected by the Confererate army in order that the plot may take its course. But the art of watching Keaton's movies is, to an unusual degree, the art of watching closely: little in *The General* is wasted, and the scenes in the recruiting office can teach us much about Keaton the actor and (to revert to a basically false but sometimes useful distinction) Keaton the director.

An extreme long shot fixes the place as downtown Marietta. Johnnie darts into the scene, but the crowds on the streets hamper his progress. He tears around a building, and then, from a new angle, reappears at the entrance of the recruiting office, first in line. When the door is opened, Johnnie, in a sense foreshadowing all the sidetracking maneuvers later in the film, proceeds resolutely on a path that doesn't happen to lead to the recruiting booth. By ignoring the custom of walking only on the floor, however, he succeeds in regaining his place in the queue. But inevitably and inexplicably, disaster follows hard on triumph. At the recruitment window, Johnnie is asked and gives his name. He also admits his occupation. The recruiter, uncertain, walks off left to consult an older man, presumably his superior, who tells him "Don't enlist him. He is more valuable to the South as an engineer." The recruiter returns to the window: "We can't use you."

Assuming he has been refused on physical grounds, Johnnie proceeds to measure himself against those who have been chosen, first a man much larger than himself, and then a more mysterious case, an elegant young man of a physique even slighter than his own, whose arms and legs the puzzled Johnnie examines and squeezes for some answer. It wasn't, he concludes, his own size or frailty that made the difference, for he moves once again in the direction of the window. The time has come for ruses. Tilting his hat over his face, he announces his name "William Brown," his occupation "Bartender." But he is soon discovered. Next he filches an acceptance paper intended for the man behind him in line as the latter looks away; but the recruiting director takes the paper back as Johnnie passes him and restores it to its owner. Now a cut to the back door: out flies Johnnie, booted by the recruiter. Rubbing his backside, he hurls his empty defiance at the whole system: "If you lose this war, don't blame me." Outside, Annabelle's father and brother, on line, invite him to join them. Still palpating his injured backside, he declines. They assume the worst.

I want to suggest three ways, all to be touched upon in connection to subsequent scenes, in which this episode seems to me to illuminate Keaton's sensibility and procedures.

(1) "Keaton's kind of reflection," J.-P. Lebel has observed in regard to another moment in *The General,* "is not at all a purely speculative one; it exists only in terms of his action, together with the careful attention he accords to the world around him, and the manifestation of his energy."[1] We've seen a hint of this quality of Keaton's typical response to the unexpected, especially to the unexpectedly unpleasant, in the scene in which Johnnie discovers that Annabelle has been following him to her own porch; we see it more clearly in the way in which he reacts to being found unsuitable for the army. The ways of destiny are never quite comprehensible; one seeks, at best, partial explanations, and these, always, not in the realm of final meanings but in the province of Things. And so Johnnie at once commences to examine his own body and the bodies of those who were accepted in order to discover an immediate physical standard by which to explain his own insufficiencies. So peremptorily does an encounter with the unexpected demand an act of physical as-

sessment that Johnnie drops all social conventions and proceeds to treat his fellow volunteers like animals on inspection at a market. Balancing Johnnie's unthinking idealism, and alone making possible the pursuit of that idealism, is the closest possible alertness to the physical world.

(2) The sequence in the recruiting office particularly reveals the range of Keaton's gestural abilities, and I am speaking for the moment not of his endlessly expressive body but of his supposedly deadpan face. The ostensible limitations of Keaton's facial repertoire disappear under even casual observation; he is "deadpan" only in that he never smiles. (More than once, to assuage uneasy producers, Keaton would produce a smile of some sort on film; one early mistake aside, the hostile reaction of preview audiences inevitably necessitated that the offending expression be changed or cut. So well accepted was his refusal to smile that he occasionally enjoyed introducing it into his films as a comic subject. In *Go West,* having accused the dealer at poker of cheating, Buster is told at gunpoint, in echo of Owen Wister's famous line in *The Virginian,* to smile when he says that. He tries, finally placing a finger at each end of his lips and stretching. But to the delight and gratification of his public, he simply can't do it.[2]) The range of facial expression in this one short sequence is quite extraordinary. As he initially waits to enlist, he projects pride and confidence (underscored by his testy response to the man behind him in line, who understandably resents the methods by which Johnnie has gotten to be first). Rejected, he shows a hurt puzzlement: why, his face asks, is this happening to *me?* When the slip of acceptance he has snatched is in turn snatched from him, he registers his impatient disappointment, somewhere between, and incorporating both, "Damn!" and *"Really!"* And then comes the look of cosmic resentment when, adding injury to insult, the recruiting officer kicks him out the door. And then, the helpless shake of the head as Annabelle's brother and father invite him into the line of re-

cruits. And then, to look ahead a bit, the face of abject defeat when he returns to The General; and then the metaphysical sadness in the great moment to come on the cross bar; and finally the twitch of amazement when he realizes that he is being rocked into a dangerous tunnel. No "pan," for anyone who bothers to look, has ever been less "dead."

(3) One quality of *The General,* unmatched in degree by any of Keaton's other features or shorts, is announced by Johnnie's repeated attentions to his bruised backside. The most agile of all screen performers, Keaton could persuade his audience that he was able to walk away unharmed from any physical punishment—spills, pratfalls, dunkings, drubbings, whatever; a quick inspection of the injured parts, perhaps a quick scratch of the head, then come what may. But in *The General,* when he is merely kicked in the rear, the immediate hurt and the cognate humiliation is richly communicated. *The General,* in other words, is the most realistic of Keaton's films—that is, the one in which what happens on the screen is nearest to what could happen if Johnnie Gray were to operate in the world of his audience. In one sense, this is hardly surprising: a good deal of realistic detail is necessary if we are to accept the extraordinary nature of the adventures to come. Another, far more elaborate expression of this same realistic impulse is the fanatical attention paid to period detail which I've already noted. But all the historical precision is, at least to me, less compelling than the more immediately human contexts in which verisimilitude is established. The distinctions between narrow- and regular-gauge tracks, between a restored but authentic nineteenth-century locomotive and a reproduction, is lost on all but a handful of viewers, but we *all* know what Johnnie is telling us when he rubs his bottom.

Annabelle's Scorn. The apparent substance of the next section of the movie, at least until its last few seconds, is so simple that it can fairly be defined by two sets of titles. The first accompanies a short scene in Annabelle's house. Annabelle asks "Did Johnnie enlist?" Her brother and father reply "He didn't even get in line" and "He's a disgrace to the South." In the second, Annabelle confronts Johnnie before The General, to which he has repaired for solace. "Why didn't you enlist?" "They wouldn't take me." "Please don't lie. I don't want you to speak to me again until you're in uniform." There isn't, in any usual dramatic sense, much more to it than that, only Johnnie's helpless defeat and Annabelle's contempt, the adolescent quality of the latter fully expressed by her "I don't want you to speak to me again." In other words, this is not the case familiar to admirers of D. W. Griffith, where the sophistication of the direction and the power of the acting are belied and often subverted by insipid titles. "When Richard Barthelmess first confronts Lillian Gish in *Broken Blossoms*," Andrew Sarris has understood, "the subtle exchange of emotions between the two players would defy the art of the greatest novelist, but the scene is almost always measured by the dime-magazine title that 'explains' it."[3] It isn't merely that Marian Mack was a less brilliant player than Lillian Gish (though she was indeed that): no actress could have made anything much more subtle or more ambiguous of Annabelle's response to Johnnie because Keaton never looks to his heroine for subtlety or ambiguity. Annabelle is and will remain one of the prettiest and most witless of Keaton's many pretty and witless young ladies. What will be fascinating to watch in later sections of the film is the growing ambivalence of Johnnie's contemplation of her childish incompetence, but at this point, thoroughly crushed, he must accept both the justice of her scorn and the unjust events which have made him its object.

Noteworthy in this passage is the interplay between Johnnie's relation to Annabelle and his relation to The General. Not surprisingly, Johnnie looks to The General for balm for the wounds inflicted by the world; returning vanquished from the recruiting office, he heads straight for his locomotive and sits on the cross bar. Suddenly he rises, but, feeling his backside, decides not to try again. Annabelle arrives, and all the time The General watches. Finally, when she leaves and Johnnie sits down once more on the cross bar, there occurs what is for many the highest point of Keaton's career, and for anyone surely one of the most breathtaking moments in the history of movies. We notice—but Johnnie does not—the assistant engineer climbing into The General. The train begins to move. Johnnie, reflecting on his grief, those great sad eyes focused somewhere beyond the limits of earthly loss, is slowly and lovingly lifted and brought down again in a series of perfect arcs. It is as if his General, according to its own awareness of his pain, were gently rocking him, giving him the physical comfort that Annabelle withholds. One love, at least hasn't deserted him.

At once irresistibly funny and achingly sad and thoroughly discomposing in its demonstration of Johnnie's ultimate helplessness, the image of Johnnie on the cross bar is one of the invaluable keys to the mystery of Buster and Things. For Things are not, as some critics would have it, invariably hostile; they are, however, invariably variable. No sooner has the remarkable image worked its full effect than we see that the loving locomotive is taking Johnnie into a dangerous narrow tunnel. His head jerks nervously back as he returns to the world, and the comfort of The General, like the prologue to the movie, is over.

The title early in the film about Johnnie's "two loves" is not, as one might at first think, frivolous or cute. Whether clambering on and off, or sitting enshrined on their cowcatchers, or, as here, finding himself rocked in their iron arms, Keaton makes known the profound sensuality of Johnnie's closeness to his locomotives. Whereas with Annabelle, his actions are often limited by the laws of chivalry, he is free with the locomotives to prove the pleasures of bodily freedom and familiarity. Johnnie's passion for his beautiful old hulks of trains—Keaton's passion for beautiful Things—gives rise to a spectacle unprecedented even in Keaton's own work and never again to be repeated. And at this point in the movie the spectacle has only just begun.

2. THE FIRST CHASE

The Plan. A title fixes the time as "a year later" and the place as "a Union encampment just North of Chattanooga." Essential to the plot but not especially interesting (and therefore very brief), this scene shows us two men in medium close-up— "General Thatcher and his chief spy, Captain Anderson"— seated at a table. "I know every foot of this railroad from Marietta to Chattanooga," says the spy, "and with ten picked men I cannot fail." He goes on, "We will enter the South as civilians coming from the neutral state of Kentucky to join the Southern cause. At Big Shanty, we will steal the train while the passengers and crew are at dinner, and proceeding North we will burn every bridge, cutting off the supplies of the Army now facing you." Thatcher answers, "Then the day you steal the train I will have General Parker advance to meet you." The plot is now clear, and the scene has done its job. Though working always from the Confederate point of view, the director doesn't bother to portray the Union officers as anything much more than a couple of moderately unpleasant-looking men.

Now, back in Marietta, we have Annabelle and her uniformed brother standing before a train; she is on her way to see "how seriously Father is injured." In a long shot, and from Annabelle's point of view, we observe the engine: it's The General and alongside, skulking about under Annabelle's contemptuous eye, is Johnnie, his face displaying a humiliation now one year old. Keaton intercuts brief medium shots of Johnnie with images of the intolerable Annabelle admiring and shining the medal on her brother's chest. Nothing has changed, including the frugality with which the director makes his point.

The train arrives at Big Shanty. Everyone descends for dinner, everyone but a group of men, all the more ominous for being seen in a perspective the reverse of that used for the other passengers, who emerge from the various coaches; one of them is Captain Anderson (who on the journey has happened to find himself seated next to Annabelle). Annabelle, noticing something missing from her purse, enters the first of two baggage cars. Johnnie is seen washing his hands in a basin outside the depot. Anderson gives the signal. The spies detach the locomotive and baggage cars from the rest of the train. Annabelle is subdued and taken prisoner. The General moves. Johnnie, his hands a mass of soapy foam, sees his General and runs after it. Others join the chase. The spies destroy the Confederate army's telegraph service. Johnnie runs on; when finally he gives up and turns to look behind him, he sees that all the others have disappeared; hands on hips, he shows his annoyed recognition that the pursuit will have to be his alone. And here commences the first of two chase sequences which are for good reason among the most celebrated ever filmed, and which, in defiance of the accepted conventions of silent comedy, come not at the end but at the very heart of the movie.

Johnnie Pursues. The first segment of the first chase is so quintessentially Keaton that, if I were instructed to locate a ten-minute passage in any of his movies that demonstrates what Keaton is all about, I'd almost surely think first of this one. It is not only the typical Keaton pursuit, it is pursuit on the most restricted and demanding terms possible, strictly confined to the lines of the railroad tracks. We have a succession of promising machines, all of which prove treasonous. We have the irony of Johnnie's being yet unaware that the train in front of him—the train at which he aims a cannon!—holds Annabelle, and the further irony of the spies believing that they are "greatly outnumbered" by a train holding one man. Finally, aside from glimpses of Annabelle and of Anderson, there are no identifiable characters other than Johnnie: unusually pure, even for Keaton, is the vision of Johnnie alone with Things.

The action develops out of Johnnie's attempt to appropriate various machines in his cause. He first sights a handcar and fits it to the track. He jumps on; it proceeds to roll backwards. He jumps off; it threatens to crush him. He climbs aboard again and begins to pump. But when it hits a stretch of track mutilated by the Union spies, the car plunges down an embankment into a river. Sighting an "ordinary"—a bicycle distinguished by a front wheel of a diameter about three times that of the rear (known more graphically in Britain as a "penny-farthing")—Johnnie literally flies onto its seat, but it clearly doesn't care for this kind of action and soon ejects its new rider. Finally—on foot—he arrives at a Southern encampment, is given a locomotive (The Texas) and a detachment of troops. As he pulls out of the camp, obsessive as usual in his attention to what lies before him, he fails to notice that the troop car remains behind.

Meanwhile, frequent cuts to The General have kept us alert to the spies' progress. Among other errands, they have stopped briefly at a water tower, but even after The General has drunk its fill, they don't bother to turn off the flow of water, with the inevitable result that Johnnie, his head stuck out the window of his new engine, is thoroughly doused as he passes beneath the tank. Once again, the Keatonian response to the mysterious is enacted: Johnnie quits the controls, looks to the skies, extends his hand palm upwards. But it isn't rain. Back at the controls, he again thrusts his head out the window and looks back. Now he understands. In Keaton's world, certain mysteries are resolved while others are not. But either way, there's no hint of any significance to all the strange accidents, and either way, one had better learn to take Things as they come.

By this point even Keaton must have been seriously challenged to cap this series of misadventures with an even more outrageous gag. What he came up with is a variant of a device he utilized in *The Navigator* two years before. In that film, protecting his ship from an army of cannibals, Buster discovers a miniature cannon which he loads and fuses. But the rope by which the cannon is drawn entwines itself about his ankle, and, whenever and wherever he turns, the cannon pursues, pointed straight at him. In *The General,* the size of both cannon and gag is exaggerated. Johnnie discovers a *real* cannon alongside the tracks and hitches it to his truncated train. First there is the problem of loading it. He measures out the powder with the scrupulosity of a French housewife adding an herb to the ragout, tamps and fuses the cannon, and scrambles back to the controls. The cannonball, unable to travel very far on such a severe diet of powder, lands at his feet. He rolls it off the train and tries the loading operation once again, this time finally nourishing the cannonball with the whole can of powder. (Looking behind him now he sees a great puff of smoke alongside the track at the point where the first ball was dumped. A new mystery: he stares into the mouth of the cannon, then, for good measure, looks to the skies. But there's no time for further reflection.) Now, however, the cannon decides to assert its independence. As Johnnie seeks to return to the cab, his foot is caught in the cannon's coupling apparatus; in the process of freeing himself he also frees the cannon from the train; now joggling self-reliantly along, it lowers its great barrel to aim directly at Johnnie, who, as in a nightmare, finds his foot caught once again, this time in a chain. Pulling free at last—after expressing his impotent desperation by hurling a stick at the cannon—he sprints over the tender and over the cab to the relative safety of the cowcatcher, for the can-

non is still pointing straight ahead. Thanks, however, to a turn
in the track, the angle of the train allows the cannon to shoot
past The Texas to The General. But that elegant machine is also
executing a turn, and the ball explodes at last just behind it as
it glides tranquilly out of danger.

Any verbal recapitulation must give the impression that this
sequence consists of a series of disasters—and so, in one sense,
it does. Yet it comes across as a single moment of pure and liberating triumph, Keaton's if not Johnnie's. Keaton's control is
here total—control of his own body, and of the accidents of time
and space, and of that most treacherously honest of machines,
the moving-picture camera. Each detail is under such sovereign
sway that one can appreciate (but I hope not accept) the position of those who find Keaton's work unpleasantly chilly. One
can, if one wishes, discern something more (or less) than human
in the flawless timing of Keaton's own movements against the
movements of machines, in the manipulation of the angles of the
two moving trains in relation to each other, in the imperturbable objectivity with which it is all photographed. But one can
also discover and know the exhilaration of sheer mastery.

Without the relief of even a momentary pause, Johnnie is
plunged into the most mysterious of all his confrontations with
Things. Having removed Annabelle, the Union spies detach the
second baggage car from The General. In order to avoid hitting
it, Johnnie switches the car to a sidetrack; then he devotes himself to some stoking. Unknown to him, the two tracks soon come
together again; when next he looks ahead the car he just dis-
posed of is looming anew before him. His contemplation of this
enigma is shortly interrupted: something has gone wrong with
The Texas, for the controls have become too hot to touch. He
rummages around for a wrench (in the course of the search
coming upon a top hat and formal coat, which, in the midst of
all the imminent peril, he examines with the attention always re-

served for new and unexpected Things), finds it, makes the repair. Meanwhile, the audience is shown the detached car being nudged off a bending track by a log deposited by the Union raiders. The repairs made, Johnnie once again confronts the problem of the disengaged baggage car. But this time it isn't there for him to see.

Keaton's love of the mischief inherent in Things gives rise to this extended gag, but it is Keaton's face that makes it unforgettable. Those great piercing eyes twice register a situation that smacks of magic. Even so, Keaton's fundamental premise remains operative: this is the real world, the world of Things, and whatever can be understood can be dealt with; to see is to solve. He blinks, as if squeezing the film from his eyes, tilts his head forward, finally tries a couple of quick glances left and right. But what Lebel defines as the transition from "tense energy" to "intense reflection" brings forth nothing, and so he "looks behind him once again and, the verifications done, returns to the driver's seat, all the tense energy . . . concentrated on the chase."[4] Johnnie lacks the time, and Keaton the temperament, for much speculation. When Buster looks a bit anxiously to the heavens, as we observe him doing so often in his movies, it is not for an answer from the gods but just to see—to see, for example, what new Thing might be unexpectedly descending toward his head.

Now the spies dump two logs on the tracks. Johnnie descends to fetch the first, but The Texas chooses to ignore its brakes and scoops him up in its cowcatcher. In another of those reversals necessary to Keaton, Johnnie's absurd new position becomes the vehicle of an elegant little victory: having unwedged the first log, Johnnie, as if playing Brobdingnagian tiddledy-winks, tips the second log off the track with the first and thereby coolly disposes of both at once. But by now the spies have had a chance to throw a switch, and The Texas is sidetracked. Johnnie reverses it, but once back on the right track it stalls for lack of traction; Johnnie jumps off, and, facing the camera but not The Texas, tosses dirt on the tracks. Absorbed by his work, annoyed by the uncooperative land, he neglects the train, which, for reasons all its own, decides to start moving. In a moment Johnnie finds himself lavishing a handful of dirt on a bare track. Once more, but not for the last time, Johnnie must chase his own train.

After a few further mishaps—among them a short sequence in which the spies set afire and detach the remaining baggage car, which The Texas, its engineer reaching a state of near-asphyxiation, must nudge through a tunnel, followed by a small misunderstanding between Johnnie and The Texas's waterhole—Keaton introduces another, far more extended and complex gag based on Johnnie's myopic absorption with his labors. Now, however, the treatment is so much richer and more extended that it calls for more specific analysis.

It works like this:

> 1. Title: "The Southern army facing Chattanooga is forced to retreat."
> 2. (long shot) The Southern commander and another officer. Before a vast background of trees and hills, he orders the retreat.
> 3. (medium shot) The cab of The General. Anderson and another spy confer.
> 4. (medium long shot) The tender of The Texas. The perspective is from slightly higher and further back on the tender. Johnnie climbs up from the cab and proceeds to chop some fuel.
> 5. (extreme long shot) The Confederate army. One Southern officer on horseback moves from the left into the frame: others appear, then the full army. The Texas, much closer to the camera, sweeps across the screen from the right, with Johnnie working away on the tender. After The Texas has passed out of the frame to the left, its steam for a time obscures the Southern troops. The army slowly returns to

view. Through all this, the camera has remained stationary.

6. (m.l.s.) Johnnie on the tender (same set-up as 4). He chops. The troops are seen moving behind him—or rather, between him and a deep landscape of trees, hills, even, in the distance, houses.

7. (l.s.) Front view of the advancing troops. The foreground is dominated by one covered wagon.

8. (m.l.s.) Johnnie on the tender. He continues to chop. From this angle, no troops are visible.

9. (m.l.s.) Johnnie on the tender. Once again, the army moves in the background. His axe becomes lodged in a piece of wood.

10. (l.s.) The tender of The General. Suddenly the heads and torsos of a dozen or so spies appear above it and from within the cab.

11. (m.l.s.) Johnnie on the tender. Since the set-up is that of 8, the army is once again not seen.

12. Title: "General Parker's victorious Northern army advancing."

13. (e.l.s.) An army in darker uniform moves against a background similar to that of 6.

14. (m.l.s.) Johnnie on the tender but from a new camera angle; The Texas is now seen directly parallel to the horizon. Johnnie chops. Once again, a single horseman—but in blue, of course—appears alone against the background; another follows, then a whole army.

15. (m.l.s.) The cab and tender of The General. The Union spies cheer.

16. (m.s.) The cab of The General. Anderson changes to a blue tunic.

17. (m.l.s.) Johnnie on the tender (same set-up as 8 and 11). His axe handle breaks almost at the blade. He races down to the cab to toss the useless handle into the stoker. Back on the tender, he tries to work with the awkward stump but soon throws it down in disgust. He moves higher on the tender to gather some wood.

18. (m.l.s.) Johnnie on the tender (same set-up as 14). In the process of gathering his fuel, Johnnie looks before him.

19. (l.s.) Union troops. But the point of view is now Johnnie's: they're on the *other* side of The Texas.

20. (m.l.s.) Johnnie on the tender (same set-up as 14 and 18). Johnnie turns to stare at the army *behind* him. He descends from the tender to the cab. For the first time in this sequence, the camera moves slightly in order to follow him.

21. (m.s.) Johnnie in the cab. He sits, facing the camera, his back to the controls. His eyes, moving left and right, reflect his situation. He rests his cheek on the palm of his right hand.

The enactment of Johnnie's recognition is marvelously subdued; Keaton's unimpeachable theatrical instincts dictate that the wonder and terror of the moment prove so overpowering—not only has fate played a filthy trick of deception but also Johnnie is now, heaven help him, in Union territory—that understatement is the only adequate rhetorical device. But everything about the scene works perfectly, and one can easily see why this sort of gag in general, and this scene in particular, were such favorites of Keaton's. Though deriving from everyone's ability to focus on a tree and miss the forest, the humor here is essentially Keaton's because essentially cinematic: devices intrinsic to the medium do it all. Ironically, Johnnie's task *seems* as important as the Southern retreat and Northern advance because the director helps make it so; the dramatic urgency of Johnnie's broken axe and his subsequent determination to make do is indeed as great as that of a strategic turning-point in the war. The essence of the gag, in sum, is the degree of *our* participation in Johnnie's obsession.

Most of the crucial shots make their contribution to this effect. In 5, as I've suggested, thanks to the steam Johnnie isn't alone in his inability to see the troops behind him. The set-up for 8, 11, and 18 restricts our perspective like Johnnie's to the work at hand. Moreover, though I've labeled 14 and 19—these frames provide some of the most frequently reproduced stills of Keaton's work—medium long shots of Johnnie on the tender. I could as accurately have identified them as deep-focus extreme long shots of the Northern troops with Johnnie incidentally dominating the foreground: there is no clear differentiation of figure and ground, no simple and definitive way of organizing the visual experience, for the two major elements are equally commanding. In addition, the vastness of the natural landscape prevents the troops from appearing as overwhelming in relation to one man and one locomotive as they might. Finally, Keaton utilizes the very silence of his medium. In a sound film even vaguely satisfying the rules of reality, the noise of hundreds of men and horses and wagons would not only be heard over the sound of a steam engine but would obliterate the noise of Johnnie's axe striking wood; in a silent film, we, like Johnnie, are free not to hear a whole army going by. Even though we see what Johnnie doesn't and laugh at his compulsive chopping, we are, if we stop to consider it, at least to some degree the secret sharers of his folly.

In their final attempt to shake Johnnie off their trail, the spies drop firewood from atop a trestle on The Texas as it passes below. Only now do they realize that "There is only one man in that engine." Johnnie, at last submitting to the urgings of self-preservation, puts on his newly-found top hat, seizes the matching coat, deserts The Texas and escapes into a forest. Alone, he observes a great shadow passing across the sky. Nature itself collaborates in his defeat by subjecting him to a storm. So, in misery, ends the chase.

3. JOHNNIE RESCUES ANNABELLE

At Union Headquarters. "In the enemy's camp," reads the title, "hopelessly lost, helplessly cold and horribly hungry." But far more eloquent than this insistent alliteration is Keaton's visualization of Johnnie's plight. We first see him tearing through the forest like a desperate animal. He turns and flies out of view at the left of the frame. A second shot sets up the new boundaries of his action: at the right of the screen the shadows of the forest, at the left the glow of the windows of the Union headquarters with their promise of warmth and food. Johnnie bounds into view at the right; he trips, but the force of his fall is at once converted into the first phase of a dazzling slide that propels him all the more efficiently toward the lighted window, his chin finally resting on the sill as he peers inside. An audible gasp has greeted this moment at every public viewing of *The General* I've attended, and with good reason. But Keaton's acrobatic skills, however breathtaking in themselves, are always at the call of the larger expressive demands of his narrative. When, in a single headlong, reckless gesture, Keaton's body challenges and subdues the entire field of cinematic space between the gloomy forest and the bright windows, it not only makes known its own powers but just as clearly announces the degree of Johnnie's frantic determination.

Entering through another window—which, to Johnnie's terror then slams shut—he finds a table laden with food, to which he helps himself. But the table is to be the scene of a meeting of Union officers and Johnnie must hide beneath it. The episode now alternates between gag and exposition: on the one hand Johnnie, almost in close-shot range, fighting off a sneeze, tormented by the pounding of one officer's fist on the table, kicked by another, and burned by the cigar held by a third; on the other hand the officers in medium shots, detailing their plans ("At nine o'clock tomorrow morning our supply trains will meet and unite with General Parker's army at the Rock River Bridge. Then the army, backed by our supply trains, will advance for a surprise attack on the rebels' left flank. Once our train and troops cross that bridge, nothing on earth can stop us"). To

Johnnie's astonishment, Annabelle is escorted in ("This girl was in the baggage car when we stole the train, so I thought it best to hold her"), then led out to be imprisoned in a bedroom. The meeting breaks up, and Johnnie sneaks out to rescue his love.

The gag of the man concealed under a table is today almost disagreeably familiar. The sneeze and the boots, though conventional enough (I can't say with certainty how conventional they looked in 1926) do achieve some fresh interest through the subtlety of Keaton's acting, but it is the cigar that brings us sharply back to Keaton's unique style. Burning through the tablecloth into Johnnie's arm, the cigar lifts an old gag to an immediacy and intensity from which most comedians would flee. The glowing tip of the cigar and its contact with Johnnie's arm are recorded with such painful clarity that Johnnie's hurt and resentment, his knitted brow, his quick rubbing of the injured spot, are in their effect something other than simply humorous. *The General* moves us close, very close, to a man living in his body, and Keaton's camera refuses to lie.

The cigar burn literally opens up other perspectives as well, for through the hole in the tablecloth Johnnie perceives Annabelle. This moment has elicited a good deal of attention. With characteristic economy it reasserts, after the considerable time they've been apart, Johnnie's adoration of Annabelle: with her face isolated and framed in the cloth in an effect very like that of an iris shot, she appears (in Sarris's words) "as in a locket tintype,"[5] or perhaps, to carry the point a bit further, as in an ikon. But just as noteworthy are the previous and subsequent shots which fill the iris with the image of Keaton's eye. Startlingly, the romantic shot of Annabelle is contrasted with the almost clinical pictures of an eye simply staring. Without denying Annabelle as an object of wonder and love, Keaton emphasizes the cold accuracy of Johnnie's—and the camera's—perception; blind worship and clarity of vision are part of a sin-

gle, richly paradoxical cinematic assertion. In this way, one simple reverse-angle device sets up one conflict which is to figure
significantly in the coming section of the movie: Johnnie as wor-
shipper vs. Johnnie as pragmatist, Annabelle as idol vs. Annabelle as clod.

Escape. Keaton's clean and classical style is expressed not only
in his use of the camera but also in his sense of narrative. At this
point in the film he proceeds to retell his story—but backwards:
now it is Johnnie who abducts both Annabelle and The General and, warmly pursued by Union forces, makes his way back
to the Confederate camp. *The General* is the most symmetrical
of screen comedies, the purest embodiment of Keaton's stated
ideals of clarity and dramatic logic.

Compelled now by forces even stronger than cold and hun-
ger, Johnnie sets out on his mission of rescue. He crawls out of
the meeting-room, briskly and coolly disposes of two sentries
(appropriating the uniform of the first) and makes his way to
Annabelle's room. He enters by the window. Annabelle is asleep
on the bed. Afraid that she may scream and give them away,
Johnnie decides to awaken her by clamping his hand over her
mouth. Now a couple of encounters with Things: repeatedly
cautioning Annabelle to be silent, Johnnie knocks over a table;
no sooner has he scrambled out than this window too slams shut
on his hand. So far we are in familiar Keaton territory. But now
Annabelle, her bodily ponderousness the antithesis of Johnnie's elegance, passes lumpily through the reopened window into
Johnnie's arms, and down they both go. Earthbound and un-
elastic, Annabelle is and will continue to be both literally and
figuratively a weight around Johnnie's neck, the accomplice of
Things.

Back in the forest, a series of terrors, including a bolt of
lightning that blasts a nearby tree and a confrontation with Kea-

ton's favorite four-legged menace, a huge bear. But Johnnie must now begin to recognize that it is Annabelle herself who most immediately threatens their escape. Unmindful of the nearly impenetrable darkness and of her complete dependency on Johnnie, she darts off insanely at every new fright, until Johnnie has to apply a flying tackle to keep her at his side. The worst occurs when she steps into an animal trap. Johnnie frees her, but in the process is himself caught, first by the hand, then by the foot. The elaborate, maddening operation of extricating himself from the trap is so satisfying an instance of Keaton's combat with Things that, at least on first viewing, one might ignore Annabelle in the background. But Keaton places in any frame only that which is worth looking at. Totally uninterested in Johnnie's extraordinary struggle with the infernal Thing, Annabelle attends to nothing but her own injured ankle. Her absolute selfishness is the natural concomitant of her absolute clumsiness, and both derive from her absolute lack of Johnnie's saving gift, his ability no matter what to achieve some kind of significant contact with the world outside himself. By this point, it seems to me, Annabelle is beginning to look less amusing than before.

Nor does she come off much more attractively in the next little scene. Johnnie decides "We had better stay here till daybreak to see where we are." As they settle in, the potentially cloying young lady of the opening is with us once more: "It was so brave of you to risk your life, coming into the enemy's country just to save me." Annabelle's face and gestures mirror the saccharine style of her words; even here she automatically falls back on flirtation and coyness. The charm of Keaton's miming of Johnnie's puzzlement at her words and subsequent mock modesty does not, I think, quite dispel the unpleasantness hovering about the edges of the scene. Here is the antebellum lady from another point of view, her essential falsity and silliness set off against the landscape of mortal danger.

Morning. The image of Johnnie and Annabelle which closes the preceding scene—both sitting upright, he holding her in his arms, his cheek against her chaste brow—is now reviewed in the light of dawn. From somewhere beyond the frame a pine cone falls—on Johnnie's head, of course. He awakens, glares resentfully at the unexpected missile, looks upward (there could be more), and scrupulously touches the bruise under his cap. Annabelle too awakens, and Johnnie pays still another tax on his passion: agonizingly he tries to unfold the bent leg on which he has rested the whole night long so as not to disturb his beloved. Once again in this episode, Keaton's pantomimic eloquence is paramount, and once again the sardonic title—"After a nice, quiet refreshing night's rest"—is no more than a feeble gloss on the arresting visual text.

Now we share Johnnie's renewed sense of danger and of outrage: not only are he and Annabelle on the enemy's grounds but there, in the middle of the camp, even in its hour of captivity looking as haughty as a great thoroughbred, stands the plundered General. Johnnie is inspired to his most daring ploy: Annabelle is to be stuffed into a sack; Johnnie (still in Northern uniform) will carry her to The General; reaching out from the sack, she is to unpin The General and the baggage car from the rest of the train; Johnnie will deposit Annabelle with the baggage and supplies, steal back The General, and return to Southern lines with warning of the coming offensive. Somehow it all works, despite a lovely little incident in which Johnnie, having stolen and emptied a sack filled with shoes, steps out of his own shoe and then can't locate it among all the others; and despite his backing into a tree which he takes for a Union sentry; and despite the near-impossibility of getting Annabelle into the sack—and how directly to the point that she be tossed about in this way, for by now it's plain that her body is no more than another intractable Thing in Johnnie's path; and despite Johnnie's hands-over-eyes horror at the sight of crates being heaved in on top of Annabelle; and despite the presence in The General of Union soldiers, all but one of whom Johnnie dispatches from the engine. We notice, if we look closely, that this one remaining man, unconscious on the floor of the cab, is the conniving Thatcher himself; but Johnnie himself isn't aware that his triumphant scheme will bring under Confederate sway *two* important Generals.

4. THE SECOND CHASE

The General Pursued. I've already noted that Keaton sets up the second chase as nearly as possible as a mirror of the first. The General has been abducted. Annabelle is in the baggage car. Union men under Anderson's command pursue in The Texas. The route is unavoidably the same. And Johnnie's first act is to destroy telegraph service. But Johnnie does his enemies one better, for he not only interrupts their means of communication but, with the help of The General's power and his own ability to move like lightning across the top of the train, he also pulls the telegraph pole down onto the tracks. The hero as game is even more wily and inventive than the hero as hunter.

Now is the moment to liberate Annabelle, and Johnnie chops a kind of window into the baggage car and scrambles through. A new dilemma: how among all the sacks to decide which one is called Annabelle? Johnnie finds the answer: step on her and she'll make herself known, and by this accident Annabelle— still idiotically clutching the pin she removed from the train, which Johnnie snatches from her and hurls to the floor—is freed. But maneuvering her body through the improvised window to the cab is no minor enterprise: her obstinate fleshiness reasserts itself almost to the point of snapping Johnnie's neck. But Annabelle's is not the only body that now calls for attention:

The General wants food, and—after a cut to The Texas which shows the Union soldiers still struggling with the pole on the tracks—Johnnie allows himself a few moments to gather some fuel.

What distinguishes all that occurs during this second chase is the much intensified sense of the urgency of the clock; each second brings a trainload of Union soldiers one second closer, so that the demands of physical space, by Keaton's axiom unimaginable in themselves, are now underscored by the no less insistent claims of time. As a result, Johnnie's attempt to garner firewood is almost as unbearable as it is delicious. Helping himself to a woodpile near the tracks, he hurls several pieces toward the tender; but there are, he discovers, some wooden objects that elect to come right back down at him, and some that like to dislodge a few of their new companions on the tender, and some that prefer to fly straight to the other side of the train. Time is nothing to independent Things.

Concentrating as ever on his job, Johnnie fails to observe until ready to start the train that Annabelle has ambled off on a task of her own: she has, he finds as he pursues her, joined two saplings, one on each side of the track, by a thin rope—hoping to halt a locomotive moving at full speed! Johnnie sardonically tests the feeble snare, acts out a tiny scene of exasperation, grabs her and hurries to the cab. The audience shares Johnnie's reaction to Annabelle's device, even feels relieved that he has begun to acknowledge her obtuseness. But we must learn never to forget or to underestimate Keaton's irony. By a quick cut to the advancing Texas just seconds earlier, the director has unobtrusively alerted us to the possible efficacy of Annabelle's idiotic invention. For we've been shown several armed soldiers hanging on to the outside of The Texas in order to take aim on The General; and Annabelle's rope succeeds beautifully in lashing the men to the sides of The Texas, immobilizing them. Like

any great ironist, Keaton is always a step ahead of both his pro-
tagonists and his audience: not only is there an ironic discrepancy between the function intended for the trap and its actual
achievement but also a further ironic discrepancy between Johnnie's (and our) smug certainty that Annabelle can do no right
and the inescapable fact that Things *will* work in their own mysterious ways. And finally, the image of the Union men struggling
and squirming in their grotesque bondage is the succinct ironic
exemplification of the hazards and indignities of pursuing Buster
Keaton through the world of Things.

Johnnie's telegraph pole and Annabelle's snare notwithstanding, The Texas has soon nearly overtaken them. With the
sides now reversed, the game of clutter-the-tracks is replayed.
Johnnie hacks furiously at the rear wall of the baggage car; it
falls and The Texas is compelled to stop. Then he unloads the
contents of the car, a series of barrels and crates; again, we see
the Union soldiers clearing their path. In the meantime, while
Annabelle mans the controls, the long-forgotten Union officer
on the floor of the cab begins to stir. But Johnnie, returning over
the tender, inadvertently knocks down a log which returns the
officer to unconsciousness. Johnnie, now (like us) reminded of
the officer's presence, appropriates his pistol, and, almost simul-
taneously, discovers an inexplicable gray military tunic (which
we recognize as the one Anderson removed when entering Union
territory). But even amid all this activity and mystery, when The
General arrives at a water tower its thirst must be attended to.

Gags based on water towers recur throughout Keaton's movies: those immense contraptions, their contents ready to explode
at a touch, are perfect embodiments of Keaton's sense of the la-
tent energies compressed in machines. (These gags, like so many
others, in fact entailed considerable risk: a water tower scene in
Sherlock, Jr. broke Keaton's neck, though his physical state apparently was such that he learned of the fracture only some years

later.) This time the principal victim is Annabelle: Johnnie, once more monomaniacally intent on the job before him, fails to notice that the spout he has fitted to The General is hanging loose from the tower and that Annabelle, only inches away, is the actual recipient of the torrent pouring unchanneled from the tower. But all at last is under control, The General is watered and on its way, and, best of all, the men on The Texas are inundated when they pass beneath the spout, for Johnnie, remembering his drenching during the first chase, has scrupulously neglected to turn off the water.

Against the epic drama of the chase we now focus on the domestic drama of Johnnie's growing familiarity with his darling dolt. Assigned to help with the stoking, Annabelle selects a piece of wood of respectable dimensions, but when her scrutiny discerns an unsightly knothole, our punctilious heroine tosses it from the train. A quick cut to the approaching Texas underscores the dangers of her idiocy. But now she surpasses even herself: unable to discriminate between playing war and playing house, she lays hold of a broom and commences to tidy up the locomotive. Johnnie hurls at Annabelle we know not what angry words. She returns to stoking, daintily adding a small stick to the fire. In a purely sardonic gesture, Johnnie gallantly offers Annabelle a fragment of wood not much larger than a toothpick. Irony, however, is lost on Annabelle, who drops Johnnie's gift into the stoker as if it might actually produce some effect there. The conflict between his tension and energy and her blockishness of mind and body produces an unavoidable explosion: in a gesture as startling as it is gratifying, Johnnie's hands fly to Annabelle's neck and he proceeds to throttle her. Then, no less suddenly, he relaxes, plants a kiss on her mouth, and returns to his work.

This pairing of incongruous gestures has been the subject of considerable comment. Sarris, who debatably takes Johnnie's

strangling of Annabelle as "a mock gesture" rather than a genu-
ine if momentary impulse, proclaims the subsequent kiss "one
of the most glorious celebrations of heterosexual love in the history of the cinema," and goes on to draw from it a definition of
Keaton's overall sense of his heroines: "Unlike Chaplin, Keaton
does not idealize women as projections of his own romantic fan-
tasies. Keaton is more like Chabrol in *Les Bonnes Femmes*
in perceiving the beauty of women through all their idiocies
and irritations. Their beauty and their indispensability. Keaton
accepts woman as his equal with clear-eyed candor, whereas
Chaplin's misty-eyed mysticism is the façade of a misogynist."[6]
Sarris's words, it seems to me, establish something like the op-
posite of their intended point: a man who repeatedly demonstrates "idiocy" and "irritation" as the signal qualities of women
may in the end prove a shade misogynistic; and after all, one
could acknowledge the "beauty" and "indispensability" of, say,
horses, without conceding them to be "equal" to human males.
By Sarris's logic, the very fact that Keaton refuses to idealize his
women—that indeed by having them act not as goddesses but
as helpmates and *then* regarding their inadequacy with "clear-
eyed candor"—somehow exonerates him from the charge of mi-
sogyny. But there are ways and ways of hating women, or at
least of looking down on them: and, in truth, Keaton as a rule
demonstrates considerable scorn for the abilities of the female
body and mind; in truth, his women tend precisely to be "projections of his own"—or at least of his heroes'—"romantic fan-
tasies," creatures wildly beloved for reasons no more substantial
than Annabelle's own passion for the Confederacy. The Keaton
woman—whether Annabelle Lee, or the heroine of *College*
who won't love Buster until he earns athletic honors, or the heroine of *Battling Butler* who won't love Buster until he beats up
the lightweight champion of the world—has, as a rule, been so
thoroughly conventionalized by Keaton the scenarist that only

the most simplistic responses are available to Buster the actor or to us.

But for the viewer of his films, the innately unpleasant implications of Keaton's portraits of women are not very important because, when all is said and done, the women are in and of themselves not very important. They are pretty enough, but they simply aren't very memorable. Nowhere in Keaton's work is there the counterpart of the extraordinary close-ups of Virginia Cherrill in the last scene of Chaplin's *City Lights;* nowhere does Keaton's camera seek out and dwell upon the uniqueness of the heroine as Chaplain's camera does with Paulette Goddard in *Modern Times* or Claire Bloom in *Limelight.* For Keaton, as Lebel has observed, "the woman serves as an impetus to show what he can do, to surpass himself, and therefore to show that he loves."[7] but the camera is far more likely to linger on the show than on the love, and more on the love than on the woman herself. Often foolish, often incompetent, often dangerous, woman is indeed "indispensable," but indispensable only to the Keaton hero's realization of his own possibilities. The kiss Johnnie gives Annabelle after throttling her, like the tintype in the opening scene, or like the image of her face framed in the hole in the tablecloth, tells us all there is to know about the "heterosexual love" in *The General;* conventional imagery must fill in where Keaton has no particular interest in more personal explorations.

The domestic scene in the cab of The General—the unsettling adumbration of what Johnnie's future with Annabelle holds—has been dwelt on as long as Keaton's style will permit, and an extreme long shot of the two trains speeding against a backdrop of wooded hills pulls our attention back to the great landscape of the chase. But now a second Union engine, The Columbia, somehow makes its way into the action, and with three trains at his disposal Keaton embarks on an even more outrageous series of railroad gags: the movie chase is carried to an unprecedented epic plane as Keaton effects all manner of collisions and unnatural couplings and other adventures and misadventures so bizarre and so complex as to defy verbal account. Yet, the immensity of the pieces notwithstanding, the chase remains essentially a game, an expression of child-like delight in pursuit and evasion. Though the complex (and exceedingly hazardous) locomotive choreography could only have issued from an obsessive regard to detail and a profound awareness of the technical possibilities of the engines, the chase is informed by the spontaneous spirit that Keaton brought to the movies from his vaudeville days. Nowhere else in screen comedy is technology so compatibly married to improvisation as in Keaton's best work.

Thanks, however, to Annabelle, all Johnnie's victories are finally offset by frustration. While he attends to bending a rail so that The Texas, temporarily sidetracked, won't be able to proceed even after regaining its route, The General moves. He runs after. It goes around a bend. Since they're on a hill, which the tracks circle, he dashes down the slope to the spot where The General must soon arrive. But just before Johnnie is able to board, Annabelle discovers how to reverse the engine. Back up it goes, back to the spot Johnnie has just quit—so he must run *up* the steep slope to regain his General. His "two loves," in quiet collaboration, guarantee him a life of unremitting tension. The chase may be nearly over, but life as Buster Keaton understands it goes maddeningly on.

Rock River Bridge. Always eager to introduce ironic parallels to the first chase, Keaton assigns Johnnie the task of destroying the Rock River Bridge in order to halt the Northern rail advance. An establishing shot announces that The General is already on the trestle; brought closer we see Johnnie at the left of the frame on the bridge itself, Annabelle at the right atop the tender tossing him logs (including a specimen so minuscule that Johnnie, enraged, can only aim it back at her: she's patently ineducable), and between them a growing pile of firewood. Thanks to Annabelle's inexhaustible maladroitness, this horizontal pattern determines the action of the scene, for as Johnnie empties The General's kerosene lantern over the pyre, she manages to dislodge the lit kindling log from the tender, thereby prematurely turning the pile into a great blaze set between Johnnie and The General. The obliging Annabelle moves the train forward a bit to give him room to leap over the fire, and he neatly clears it—only to sail straight through the bridge to the river below. Our astonishment at this moment is not unmixed with alarm: you don't have to be aware that in all his films Keaton himself performed virtually every stunt, no matter how dangerous, in order to feel certain that here and now, in this take, it looks like Keaton and none other sailing through the bridge and, in a second shot, hitting the water. Elsewhere in the movie— during the later battle scenes, for instance—the comedy is so fantastic that we are not especially concerned with any direct continuity between Johnnie's fictional perils and actual, immediate hazards to the actor. But in the dive from Rock River Bridge, perhaps more abruptly than anywhere else in *The General,* the camera's unclouded eye subverts our comfortable sense that Johnnie Gray isn't *really* Buster Keaton. And Keaton intensifies the hair-raising effect by holding his camera on the empty river for a few intolerable seconds before Johnnie sails into the frame and then into the water. He knew how to do the stunts, and he knew how to photograph them: perhaps such praise would have been simple enough to satisfy even a man who could write "I never realized I was doing anything but trying to make people laugh when I threw my custard pies and took my pratfalls."[8]

Once Johnnie has swum to shore, a cut to The Texas instructs us that the Union men are still fussing helplessly with Johnnie's bent rail. By now, such images of Johnnie's pursuers reduced to spluttering indignity have become familiar: doused by the water tank, preposterously bound to their own engine by Annabelle's rope, jolted senseless by a collision with The Columbia that nearly sends The Texas speeding over the edge of an unfinished inclined track, they are seen primarily as the bumbling, irate victims of Johnnie's maniacal determination to carry himself and his Annabelle and his General back home. With *The General*, screen comedy has attained such a level of lucidity and sophistication that the treatment of the Union soldiers looks almost anachronistic, an amusing historical reference to the moronic stumblings and pilings-up of primitive movie chases. But in fact the Keystone Cops were not invented a hundred years, or fifty, or even much more than ten before, and if we unthinkingly ascribe *The General* to a far later period of movie history, our error can be attributed exclusively to Keaton's imagination and skills.

At long last, The General is home: Johnnie spots a Confederate soldier and cheerfully waves. He's greeted by gunfire. This time it's Annabelle who sees what is wrong and helps him remove his purloined blue tunic. The chases end, and the battle scenes are ready to begin, as Johnnie puts on the gray uniform he was denied at the beginning of the movie—a uniform recently used to disguise a Northern spy. And besides, it doesn't fit.

5. THE BATTLE

The Return. The sequence in which Johnnie returns begins and ends with a couple of long shots paradigmatic of Keaton's use of that simple but, for him, essential directorial device. The first shot, of a Southern town in the midst of which The General appears, is a purely functional establishing shot, because the story must be told. The last is of notable beauty and haunting intimation, because the possibilities of Buster the performer must be exploited. For all its fertility, Keaton's art operates on such simple premises.

In the interim comes a series of little scenes in which Johnnie's personal animation is virtually lost amid the collective energies of an army on the move. Once he has gotten the ear of the Confederate general and announced the enemy strategy, the alarm is sounded; the machinery of battle is in motion, and Johnnie, still explaining away, looks dwarfed by the cavalry and foot soldiers running on either side. In the earlier shots of Johnnie chopping on the tender while two armies pass by unnoticed, the set-up thrusts Johnnie into prominence; here, however, in anticipation of the great moment to come, Keaton wants Johnnie to look very small indeed against the processes of war. Johnnie's ineffectuality is further stressed by his not-especially-welcome ministrations to the general (helping him on with his sword and onto his horse) and, a bit later, by another frustrating encounter with Annabelle, with whom he finds himself trapped among the charging cavalry but who, in the midst of his instructions for her safety, spies her wounded father and hurries out of Johnnie's control. Similarly, his encouragements to the troops—as if they need, or even notice, his pep-rally urgings—quickly turn into desperately self-protective thrashing gestures as the troops threaten to crush him in their progress. Keaton clearly fixes a scene, and by implication a world, from which Johnnie might as well be missing.

But Johnnie Gray can't accommodate himself to defeat. Slowly, in exquisite mime, he discovers and illustrates how one should—or, when appropriate, should not—walk through a military charge, and with some relief we observe once more Johnnie's cunning, Johnnie's indomitability. But then the set-up changes.

An army fills the screen, then moves out of sight; women and children, cheering, follow after; the town is utterly deserted, except for one motionless figure set against some of the same buildings we saw in the bland establishing shot a few minutes earlier. Schooled by abrupt recent experience, Johnnie looks behind him: at least now no more are coming. The angle shifts: we're brought somewhat closer, though still in long-shot range. In one telling composition, Keaton is showing us Johnnie's reward for his prodigious labors of the last twenty-four hours. He shoves his hands into his pockets. Then he notices a sword beside him on the road. He picks it up, and, as if stepping into trousers, attaches the belt, ready to follow the others into battle. But the instrument of his rebirth is first and foremost a Thing. Johnnie, being Buster Keaton, trips on his weapon. Johnnie, being Buster Keaton, hoists himself up, adjusts the angle of the sword, and propels himself once more into the action. Though racing in the general direction of the camera, he flies out of the frame to the left well before entering the province of the close shot. Johnnie hasn't given up, but the wise director never moves close enough to his subject to allow his camera to explore the unanswerable question of why.

The Other Side. Keaton's rather conventional handling of the Union soldiers is seen for the last time when, still fretting over the maimed rail, they stare in awe and confusion at a huge soldier who arrives as if from nowhere and, with only an axe, sets right the disorder. But the time for such relatively trivial joking is over.

A suite of extreme far shots—one of the Rock River Bridge partly aflame, several of the Union army in motion, one of The Texas approaching—tell us what we need to know: The Texas and the advancing Union forces have come together. The Union officers argue their strategy, and the commander on horseback announces to the men on The Texas that "That bridge is not burned enough to stop you, and my men will ford the river." After another shot of the bridge, the train moves past the flames —and then the bridge gives out. Amid smoke and flames, The Texas falls, still steaming as it hits the water. In medium shot, fellow officers and soldiers behind him, the man who gave the fatal command surveys his accomplishment, his expression not one of mere anger, or mere abashment, or mere pain.

There are those who find this episode funny, and Keaton himself has bestowed on it his catch-all label of "gag." To be sure, as we watch The Texas moving gracefully and powerfully onto the horizontal plane of the bridge, then watch both train and trestle crumple before our eyes, we experience something of the comic pleasure that always follows the deflation of serenity and composure and pride (and I attribute these qualities both to the train and to the officer). But I at least cannot help feeling loss (and not loss of human life alone) far more potent than any impulse to laughter; I've found myself too close to the beautiful, independent trains of *The General* to look complacently on their humiliation. Earlier I compared The General to a great thoroughbred; and The Texas, as it lies in the river, twisted and broken and desperately exhaling its steam, seems to me painfully like a noble animal stricken. This is surely the blackest joke in the history of silent movie comedy, and I can conceive of no one but Keaton who would have dared it.

However one may respond, the collapse of the Rock River Bridge again neatly exemplifies the meaningful spareness of Keaton's directorial manner. Think of David Lean's *The Bridge on the River Kwai* (1957), in which the famous climactic destruction of bridge and train happens in a flurry of cross cutting between the bridge, the British commandoes who have mined it, the approaching Japanese train, the British officer paradoxically determined to save the trestle he has built as a monument to the

courage and ingenuity of his countrymen, the Japanese commandant, and still other characters trapped in a sticky web of motives and events. Even if one finds Lean's direction unnecessar-
ily melodramatic, one has to allow that the cinematic expression
of all the issues at stake in the scene demands some athletic cutting and editing. In *The General,* on the other hand, Keaton is
satisfied with a long shot of the approaching Texas from the
shore nearest the train, a horizontal image of the bridge from a
point far downstream, held until The Texas has fallen and
writhed for a few moments, and the medium reaction shot of the
officer. It would be easy to explain away Keaton's technique as
"primitive" and so ascribe the difference between his style and
Lean's to the thirty years of history—not necessarily cinematic
history alone—that separates their work; but among Keaton's
contemporaries were, after all, Griffith and F.W. Murnau and
Erich von Stroheim, directors whose work cannot be called simple. Nor is it a question of genre: frantic cutting for the sake of
suspense is well within the given boundaries of Keaton's kind of
comedy. No, in this great scene Keaton is simply less interested
in suspense than demonstrating the inevitability of disaster in the
world of Things, and in three extended shots, free of the nervous
perturbation that would be conveyed by a succession of quick
cuts, he makes the disquieting point that since the handsome
train and the handsome bridge must indeed fall, all we can do
is wait and watch. And significantly, Keaton sees to it that Johnnie Gray isn't among the spectators; as usual it's the loser, this
time the Union commander, who must observe the irresistible
force of reversal and ruin meeting the pathetically moveable objects of this world. Where Lean uses his camera to stress the con-
trarieties of a highly-wrought plot, Keaton insists on his own
sense of earthly experience.

The sweep of Confederate triumph is ineluctable. The hap-
less Union officer orders an advance; the Confederate General

commands his troops to fire; the Union cavalry, with the slaughtered Texas lying ominously in the background, retreats across Rock River. In light and in shadow, the combat rages on. And to a degree unexampled in the history of American film, the audience feels it is indeed watching not merely some battles but, unmistakably, the Civil War itself, the great war of our schoolbooks and our imagination. The effect owes much to Keaton's fanatical concern with period detail, but finally the photography makes the difference between mere accuracy and uncanny reproduction. For as every serious commentator has duly noted, in *The General*—and most unforgettably, I find, in these battle scenes—the celebrated Civil War photographs of Mathew Brady and his assistants seem magically animated. Precisely how Keaton achieved this is a secret he and his cameramen, Dev Jennings and Bert Haines, carried to their graves. Moreover, as Vincent Canby observes, "lots of films made in the 1920s also had the Brady look, which has as much to do with styles of costumes and lighting, and with the quality of film stock, as with conscious effect."[9] In truth, there are scenes in Keaton movies not set in the Civil War which approximate the effect of Brady's still photography; that is, scenes in which the grainy image produces an effect at once analytical and lyrical, showing exactly *how* the photography works yet at the same time communicating a sense of the hovering fragility of the subject. But only in *The General* do photography and period come together to create an entire world. David Robinson is aware that "No one—not even Griffith or Huston and certainly not Fleming—caught the visual aspect of that war as Keaton did. . . ."[10] Opting for Technicolor in *Gone With the Wind* (1939), Victor Fleming (or whoever made such decisions) automatically sacrificed the Brady surface; John Huston, in *The Red Badge of Courage* (1951) pursued it so consciously and so conscientiously that, for all its visual impressiveness, his movie sometimes looks more like a sophisticated comment on Brady than the real thing, another instance of the modernist preoccupation with art as reference and homage; Griffith, in *The Birth of a Nation* (1915) and to a considerably lesser degree in *Abraham Lincoln* (1930), comes close to Keaton's achievement but, to my eye at least, doesn't match it. By some marvel, *The General* simply *is* the Civil War as Brady has trained our eyes to recognize it.

Johnnie the Soldier. Still struggling with his sword, a more willful and versatile instrument than he had suspected, Johnnie Gray returns to the foreground. As the Southern general issues commands, Johnnie echoes his words in totally wasted, unconsciously parodistic gestures. At first Johnnie seems likely to prove no less impotent and inconsequential here than in his last appearance. Repeated cuts to scenes of battle stress the emptiness of his performance, while closer shots of his ongoing contest with the sword—the blade has developed a talent for disengaging itself from the hilt—remind us that this would-be commandant isn't even capable of subduing the small, theoretically inanimate foe strapped to his own body.

Yet for the next few minutes every reversal will become the stuff of triumph. Still playing general, Johnnie decides to oversee the firing of a cannon, but to his increasing discomfiture an unseen sniper picks off one after another of his men. When all save himself are gone, Johnnie, sword in hand, shifts his command to an adjacent cannon crew, but, thanks to his magniloquent gesturing, his treacherous sword once more flies off its hilt—and impales the sniper. Johnnie is now obliged to man the first cannon solo, but finds this instrument no friendlier than the one he had earlier attached to The Texas: loaded and fused, it elects to jerk to a vertical position before firing. Where the ball will land becomes a question of rather pressing uncertainty—Johnnie's diffident glances straight upwards suggest one disquieting possibility

—but an unexpected shot of a dam exploding, and another of Union soldiers caught in the subsequent torrent, tell us that Johnnie can, for a time, do no wrong. Southern victory is in the air and Johnnie operates in a state of grace.

Hence we are ready for what will appear to be the final symbolic triumph of Johnnie the warrior. An abrupt cut shows us a soldier bearing the Confederate colors; he is hit; Johnnie darts in from nowhere, takes up the flag before it touches the ground, and without losing a step, flies to the edge of a hill where he poses in solemn testimony to Southern indomitability. Over he goes: the rock on which he has placed himself is in fact the arched back of a Confederate officer. The sequence ends with Johnnie, capsized, hearing himself upbraided by one of his own leaders. Victory, as always, is momentary, and posturing not to be tolerated.

The scenes of Johnnie in battle, with their own little dramatic structure and their own comic rhythm, could easily be excerpted from *The General* and screened to illustrate the delicate nuance of Keaton's performing style; the balance he maintains between gestures of determined bravado and glances defining a scrupulous personal caution is beautiful to remember. Indeed, these scenes might prove more satisfactory as a self-contained unit than as an episode, for, intercut with and often causally related to the Bradyesque war scenes, they seem to some, including myself, the weakest in the movie. Penelope Houston once remarked that "in the final battle scenes . . . the [comic] effects seem rather too deliberately contrived, the [combat] situations a little too real to be altogether funny. In part this may be because the film . . . conveys, so unobtrusively, so exact and stylish a sense of its period. The comedian has strayed onto a real battlefield, and momentarily the illusion cracks."[11] What's more, these scenes present Johnnie Gray largely as the creature of miraculous forces outside himself: the redeeming ingenuity and skill he could call into play during the great chases are scarcely in evidence, and there is good reason to lament both their absence and the consequent shift in comic emphasis. The over-all consistency of *The General* is such that any lapse makes itself forcefully known.

On the other hand, it might well be argued that antithesis and incongruity—between the several elements of the scene, between the scene and the rest of the film—is just what Keaton wanted: by intercutting shots of epic grandeur and epic destruction with shots of one small would-be hero in the business of staying alive, the director could be trying his hand at one simple, quintessential possibility of montage. It could be proposed that Keaton's lucid comic vision—like Stendhal's in *La Chartreuse de Parme,* like Shakespeare's in *1 Henry IV* and Welles's in *Chimes at Midnight*—here catches and records something of the vile fundamental irony of war itself. That the scene in question leaves us dissatisfied may, in short, be the point; but even if so, the terms of Keaton's argument have shifted a bit abruptly.

"Heroes of the Day." The Southern cavalry returns in triumph, led by a human mascot whom no eye but the camera's seems to notice. Poor Johnnie can do little more than wander out of the cavalry's path; predictably, he wanders into The General. After a loving touch, he climbs aboard—and his legs quite literally give out as he stumbles on the long-forgotten officer he captured at the Union encampment, now at last stirring. The discovery introduces one of Keaton's loveliest pantomimes. No one could imitate the penetrating glances, the respectful yet authoritative, incredulous yet lordly manner in which he leads General Thatcher at gunpoint to the Southern command, the punctiliousness with which he brushes the dust from Thatcher's uniform, the swagger as he delivers his unexpected trophy. Yet even at such a moment as this, Keaton's face must not express joy; in-

stead, while he watches Thatcher tender his sword to the Confederate general, the pistol in his hand suddenly goes off in unambiguous expression of his quasi-orgasmic delight.

Johnnie is finally the cynosure of the Southern camp. Now, however, as he fingers the most wonderful of Things, a Union general's sword, the Southern commandant seems to turn on him: "Is that your uniform?" "I had to wear it to get through the lines." "Take it off." Johnnie, crushed, hands over his usurped tunic. But as Annabelle and her father and all the others look on, Johnnie is presented with an incomparably more desirable costume—and with Thatcher's own weapon. "Enlist the lieutenant," the general orders. "Occupation?" And at long last the correct answer: "Soldier." A medium-close image of Keaton's splendid profile underscores Johnnie's new eminence and dignity. Annabelle rushes to him, and he leads her—where else?—to The General. There, with the lovers seated on the cross bar, the harmony of the opening is regained. The plot is over.

But not the movie. Keaton must have his final gag, and he invents one worthy of its honored place at the close of *The General*. A shot of the camp, with one soldier afoot, reminds us that Johnnie and Annabelle are not quite alone. Back to the engine: a couple of soldiers pass and naturally give the new lieutenant a salute, which he must return. Another shot of the camp; another soldier; another interruption. Then, a third and last shot of the camp shows not one but scores of soldiers being disgorged from their tents, all apparently determined to keep Johnnie from his love-making. Johnnie contrives a way out. Originally seated to Annabelle's left, he simply reverses their position on the cross bar; now his back is to the soldiers who pass, and, his left arm all the while encircling Annabelle as they kiss, his right arm jerks with piston-like regularity in perpetual, indiscriminate salute. No other ending would provide such telling irony. Part of Johnnie has found its love. The rest of Johnnie has become a machine.

summary critique

Like any notable style, Keaton's asserts itself even, and thus most decisively, in the smallest details. Three moments in *The General,* together not adding up to a full minute of cinematic time, seem to me to announce or at least imply all that is most nearly definitive of Keaton and to isolate the principal issues raised by my analysis of the film.

(1) Two bodily gestures teach the lesson of the performer. One occurs during the first chase; the precise moment is, significantly, insignificant. Buster finds himself atop the cab of The Texas. His placement offers him the clearest possible view of his situation. His feet, soles *and* heels, grip the floor. His right hand shields his eyes from the sun. His legs and torso and neck and head form an uninterrupted forward angle of, say, eighty degrees. Though the train beneath him speeds forward, the cosmos might as well have come to a full halt. Buster Keaton is trying to see.

The image echoes so many others in Keaton's work that it could well serve as trademark. In *The Three Ages,* for instance, we first see Buster the caveman in a similar posture, atop an animated dinosaur; while in a frequently reproduced still from the lost *Love Nest,*[1] he's equipped with binoculars and, legs slightly spread, hangs at a far more precipitous angle from the rigging of a ship. The background is never twice the same, for no other comedian has appropriated such a range of narrative time and place; but the instinct to look, to see, to be as sure of Things as life will ever allow, never abates. The fabulous eyes—examine

almost any still from any Keaton film—are not simply one remarkable feature of an altogether remarkable face: they are
Keaton's way of dealing with the present tense. And they are,
as we've seen, the essential clue to the identity of performer and
director.

(2) Just after his second leap onto the handcar at the beginning of the chase, Buster's torso is rigid as his arms take control
of the machine; his legs, off the floor, momentarily trace an almost balletic scissors design. He's trying, of course, to channel
whatever energy he can generate into the act of pumping the machine. But the gratuitous loveliness of his movement here ex-
presses at once the irrepressibility of his bodily energy and that
apportionment of energy we call poise.

Such moments, born of a unique coupling of grace and intensity, distinguish Keaton from all other actors; indeed, his
mastery of his body is such that, paradoxically, like the greatest
and only the greatest of dancers, he is often most fascinating in
repose. Yet for all this I find it difficult to point to the precise
sources of his bodily expressivity. These words of Edwin Denby
do, however, tell at least one important part of the story:

> [His] is an unusually thick and long neck. But its expressiv-
> ity lies in its clear lift from the trunk, like a powerful thrust.
> The shoulders are not square, but slope downward; and so
> they leave the neck easily free, and the eye follows their sil-
> houette down the arms with the sense of a line extraordinar-
> ily extended into space, as in a picture by Cézanne or
> Raphael.

Denby further notes that he distinctively "tilts his head slightly
from the topmost joint, keeping this joint mobile against the upright thrust of the other vertebrae," and mentions the way he
"alters his neck to suit [the] character" he portrays, a point I
attempted to make earlier in regard to the heroes of *The General*
and *Battling Butler*. All of this seems to me remarkably illumi-

nating of Keaton's art; but Denby happens to be speaking not of Keaton but of Nijinsky.[2] That two performers emerging from such different training and traditions and operating in such different theatrical contexts should each have developed such similar devices of expression is perhaps an accident, and at any rate a phenomenon the implications of which I am not equipped to explore; but that what an alert critic can see in a great dancer should bear such striking relevance to Keaton can stand as the definitive rejoinder to those who see Keaton's performances as enchanting but artless gambols.

But in the end all analogies to dancing fall short. First, the plasticity of Keaton's gestures are not to be understood by any grammar of movement; and second, he moves not to music but, always, to the urging of environment. His natural scene, in more than one sense of "natural," is one without limits: beyond the four edges of the screen (for dangers not only proceed from all corners of the land but can swell from underground, can fall from the skies) lie deserts of vast and ominous actuality. Well he knew what he was about when he turned down the stage of the Shubert brothers for the screen of Arbuckle: no stage space could contain the possibilities built into his muscles.

(3) Hence the central importance in Keaton's directorial technique of those long shots of all kinds which, by their very nature, communicate in a single image the sense of a man in relation to his world. But, as Penelope Houston among others has observed, Keaton's passion for the long shot satisfies other needs as well:

> [One] obvious Keaton principle is his fondness for keeping as much of the action as possible within a shot. It started, presumably, with a natural pride in letting the audience see that those leaps and falls and glissades of movement were all his own work. There could be no cutting, because to cut into the action would suggest a cheated effect. . . . He was pre-

pared to risk his neck for an effect which might last twenty seconds on the screen. The camera had to get far enough back to take it all in, to exploit a connoisseur's satisfaction in the number of ways of staging a fall.[3]

Precisely so, and the pertinence of Houston's remarks is evident throughout *The General*. But one must add that Keaton habitually employs the long-take long shot to capture actions other than stunts.

When, for example, Johnnie Gray abandons The Texas at the end of the first chase, he carries the coat and wears the top hat he unearthed in the toolbox. We have a shot of a small clearing in the forest: Johnnie rushes in from the foreground. The hat is caught in the crook of a branch and lifted from his head. Something strange is happening: he touches his skull. He looks to the ground: no hat. Still staring downward, he retraces his steps until standing once again under the branch. His head grazes the hat—so lightly that he doesn't realize it—and the hat is replaced on his head. He touches it. He takes it off. He bends away from, and stares in terror at, the branch. After a second, he throws down both hat and coat and runs—though not without one final Buster Keaton look at the apparently animated limb.

Like so many of the stunts, this little pantomime is seen from a distance. But here Keaton isn't showing off his bravery and endurance, but rather (1) providing a clever bridge between two major sequences, (2) reaffirming the mysterious relation of actor and scene, and (3) publishing, without resort to melodramatic close-ups, the timorousness Johnnie naturally feels in enemy territory, expressed as a child's terror of a spooky forest at night. This kind of directorial economy looks particularly attractive to today's movie audiences, and Houston concludes that the quite extraordinary rise of Keaton's critical stock in recent years can be attributed in part to his devotion to his long shots, to "the technique which happens to be most in line with modern, or at least 1960s, aesthetics."[4] The point seems to me well taken, and may help us see why, if silent comedy once looked like "Chaplin and the others," it is now, among critics of whatever school, "Chaplin and Keaton and the others." Indeed, were I to allow Keaton top billing—though a noisy discussion might result —very few would find my gesture eccentric.

CREATIVE INTELLIGENCE

We are, then, only now arriving at some kind of just appreciation of Buster Keaton as what Hugh Kenner has termed "a presiding creative intelligence."[5] Keaton's best work is his alone and absolutely inimitable: those who have been visibly influenced by him, most notably Jacques Tati, have come up at best with movies of varying quality that incidentally look as if their makers have been watching Buster Keaton. (Tati "is just out to be artistic": Keaton's own judgment[6] seems to me only slightly too severe.) Moreover, Keaton's physical presence so specifically calls for the kind of handling only he knew how to provide that collaboration always threatened collision; excepting Chaplin (and even here we have only the evidence of one relatively brief sequence), it's unlikely that any writer or director of marked personal vision could have worked profitably with him.

Nothing illustrates this more forcefully and more pathetically than *Film*. When the project was first announced, lovers of Keaton and lovers of Beckett all over the globe must have rejoiced: Keaton, the exemplar of pertinacity in absurd causes, seemed the ideal Beckett hero, especially in his old age; Beckett, the supreme poet of meaninglessness, would provide Keaton with his loveliest script, uncontaminated by conventional pretty heroines and happy endings. Some wise Keatonites may have been skeptical, but I doubt that even they could have predicted the actual unpalatability of the fruit of this partnership.

The scenario of *Film*—the title, by the way, beyond its more obvious implications, appears to refer to the matter covering Keaton's one exposed eye—is available for those who wish to study it; I prefer to dwell not on the movie itself but on the sources of its failure. For we should all have been able to predict that this collaboration would prove disastrous. Keaton, as we know, needed the long shot to imply among other things a world of challenging spaces; in Beckett's theatrical world the possibilities of space itself are challenged. In *Waiting for Godot,* we are not only asked whether Godot himself exists but whether the failure of Vladimir and Estragon to go anywhere at the end of the play announces that there is, beyond the four corners of the stage, no place to go. In *Endgame,* Beckett's most generous theatrical statement, Hamm and Clov recognize that their game —call it competition, call it drama—can be played out only within the limits of their walled world: *is* there something called "nature" beyond those notorious windows? Buster Keaton was clearly unwilling to listen to such questions, and so he lurches through *Film*—Alan Schneider's thoroughly insensitive camera usually tracking him, and from the rear!—without any sense of what he's failing to understand. On the other hand, the availability of a real clown appears somehow temporarily to have anesthetized Beckett's marvelous alertness to the theatricality of all human dealings; he gives old Keaton no business remotely worthy of him. Two of the funniest men who ever lived turn grim in each other's presence.

What's more, Beckett in *Film* so misjudges his material as to stint on those moments in which we're shown Keaton's successes in his perpetual encounter with Things—even though such scenes, with their juncture of victory and absurdity, make a point on which Beckett himself has never hesitated to dwell.

In one sense more Beckett than Beckett himself, for instance, is the contrast provided by two sequences of *The Navigator*. A very rich and spoiled young man (Buster) and a very rich and spoiled young woman find themselves alone and adrift on an ocean liner. On their first morning aboard, the forlorn couple enters the galley. The larder is full; there is, to all appearances, no question of starvation. But eggs and bacon and cans of food are after all Things. Some of the difficulties they face in making nourishment of Things depend on the relatively simple limitations of their experience: you don't make a good cup of coffee, the naive millionaires discover, by scrupulously measuring four unground beans into a massive pot, filling it with sea water, and letting it boil away. But far more serious is Buster's burden of opening cans. The keys attached to the cans of course don't work. Various sharp-edged instruments are conscripted, but the first draws nothing more than packing liquids from the can and the second engenders a pair of dangerous missiles as it splits the can in two. Buster does no better with the eggs, dropped into a vat of boiling water so immense that their recovery is nearly impossible. The first breakfast is a disaster.

The second breakfast sequence—"weeks later," as the title tells us, they're still afloat—shows us a triumph. By now the galley, as Robinson nicely describes it, "is a forest of levers and pulleys and wires, all the business of living neatly mechanized. A lever fills the coffee-pot with coffee and water and puts coals on the fire. A saw, improvised out of a grindstone and handsaw, opens tins and files [Buster's] nails in one operation. A cage lowers eggs into the giant cooking pot which had earlier given such trouble; and a further series of levers and pulleys sets the table."[7] By these extravagant means—and, implicitly, *only* by such extravagant means—can coffee get made, cans opened, eggs boiled, tables set. If Things won't willingly cooperate in our service, they must be trapped and controlled by ingenuity. Give them the most minute degree of freedom, it appears, and they will revert to their surly savage state; a harshly colonialistic policy is our only hope of dealing with the monsters. Keaton's galley proclaims both the bizarre results of human cunning and the necessity of resorting to cunning in the first place: what we see is a fantastic dream born of the nightmare of Things. And such visions were only possible when Keaton was free to work on his own terms.

Similarly, only Buster Keaton could have dreamed up the final image of *The General,* in which Johnnie Gray, now the great hero and now the great lover, salutes and kisses and salutes and kisses all in the same instant. It turns out that we look hardly less silly when we succeed than when we don't, but if all else fails (and all else always fails) we take what pleasure we can in our absurdly provisional victories. Keaton's subject—like Chaplin's, though so differently perceived—is survival: we try to live despite all our enemies, we try to live despite all our pride. André Malraux once said that, after the experience of the prison camps of World War II, the only books that still seemed true were *Don Quixote, Robinson Crusoe,* and *The Idiot;*[8] I wonder if the best work of Buster Keaton might not be allowed to join this company, for it too faces up to the finally hilarious predicament of a queer little man who refuses to give in to the inevitable one second before his time.

a Keaton filmography
bibliography
rental sources
purchase sources
notes

a Keaton filmography

I list only the silent films in which Keaton appeared. The complete filmography, running to 124 items, has been compiled by Raymond Rohauer and Rudi Blesh and appears in Blesh's *Keaton*. I have drawn on this list as well as on the one David Robinson includes in his *Buster Keaton*.

1. THE ARBUCKLE SHORTS

All directed by Roscoe Arbuckle, produced by Joseph M. Schenck for Comicque Film Corporation, and released through Paramount Famous Players-Lasky.

1917 *The Butcher Boy, Rough House, His Wedding Night, Oh, Doctor, Coney Island*
1918 *Out West, The Bell Boy, Moonshine, Goodnight, Nurse, The Cook*
1919 *A Desert Hero, Back Stage, The Hayseed, The Garage*

2. METRO FEATURE

1920 *The Saphead* (directed by Herbert Blaché, produced by John L. Golden)

3. KEATON PRODUCTIONS SHORTS

All directed by Keaton and Eddie Cline, except *The Goat and The Blacksmith* (Keaton and Malcolm St. Clair) and *The Love Nest* (Keaton alone), produced by Schenck, and released by Metro (the first eight) and First National (the last eleven).

1920 *The High Sign, One Week, Convict 13, The Scarecrow, Neighbors*
1921 *The Haunted House, Hard Luck, The Goat, The Electric House* (not completed), *The Playhouse, The Boat, The Paleface*

75

1922 *Cops, My Wife's Relations, The Blacksmith, The Frozen North, Day Dreams, The Electric House* (completed version), *Balloonatics*
1923 *The Love Nest*

4. KEATON PRODUCTIONS FEATURES

All produced by Schenck, released by Metro (the first seven) or United Artists (the last three). Official directorial credit given in parentheses.

1923 *The Three Ages* (Keaton and Cline), *Our Hospitality* (Keaton and Jack G. Blystone)
1924 *Sherlock Jr.* (Keaton), *The Navigator* (Keaton and Donald Crisp)
1925 *Seven Chances* (Keaton), *Go West* (Keaton)
1926 *Battling Butler* (Keaton), *The General* (Keaton and Clyde Bruckman)
1927 *College* (James Horne), *Steamboat Bill Jr.* (Charles "Chuck" Reisner)

5. METRO-GOLDWYN-MAYER PRODUCTIONS

1928 *The Cameraman* (directed by Edward Sedgwick Jr., produced by Keaton)
1929 *Spite Marriage* (directed by Sedgwick, produced by Schenck)

bibliography

1. BIOGRAPHIES AND INTERVIEWS

Unless otherwise noted, all my biographical information is drawn from these sources.

Bishop, Christopher, "An Interview with Buster Keaton," *Film Quarterly,* XII, 1 (Fall 1958), 15–22. Reprinted in *Interviews with Film Directors,* ed. Andrew Sarris. New York: Avon Books, 1969, 274–286.

Blesh, Rudi. *Keaton.* New York: Macmillan, 1966. The "definitive"—and fascinating—biography, based largely on interviews with Keaton and his intimates. Some weaknesses, but indispensable.

Brownlow, Kevin. "Buster Keaton, An Interview," *Film* 42 (Spring 1965), 6–10.

Feinstein, Herbert. "Buster Keaton sur le vif," *Cahiers du Cinéma* 175 (février 1966), 11–12.

Friedman, Arthur B. "Buster Keaton: An Interview," *Film Quarterly,* XIX, 4 (Summer 1966), 2–5.

Gillett, John, and James Blue. "Keaton at Venice," *Sight and Sound,* XXXV, 1 (January 1966), 26–30.

Keaton, Buster. "A Quatre Temps," *Cahiers du Cinéma* 130 (avril 1962) 29–33. Transcription of an interview; interviewer and translator anonymous.

Keaton, Buster, "with" Charles Samuels. *My Wonderful World of Slapstick.* London: George Allen and Unwin, 1967. (Since the U.S. edition–New York: Doubleday, 1960—is out of print, I refer throughout to the British edition.) The poisonous title and the suspicious "with" of the credits tell the sad story: this is undiluted show-biz bio, often repulsive in style and far less accurate than Blesh's book. Still, it's BK's own version of his life and so not to be ignored.

Nizan, Henriette. "Portrait de Buster Keaton," *Le Magasin du Spectacle* 4 (août 1946), 66–76. A Frenchwoman's account of her encounters with the spectre of "le grand Buster" during her residence in Hollywood in the 1940s: very affecting.

Schmitz, John. "Une rencontre avec Buster Keaton," traduit de l'américain par Jean-Pierre Coursodon, *Cahiers du Cinéma* 86 (août 1958), 15–17.

2. CRITICISM

Agee, James. "Comedy's Greatest Era," *Life* (September 5, 1949), 70–88. Reprinted, among other places, in *Film: An Anthology,* ed. Daniel Talbot. Berkeley: University of California Press, 1970, pp. 130–47. Perhaps the most celebrated essay on silent comedy, among its virtues are some lovely pen-portraitures of BK.

Benayoun, Robert. "Le Colosse de silence," *Positif* 77–78 (été 1966), 18–24. Keaton meets Kafka: the treatment is less than persuasive.

———. "Le Regard de Buster Keaton," *Positif* 77–78 (été 1966), 1–17. Observations on BK's eyes lead to a generally undistinguished and not always accurate biographical essay.

Bishop, Christopher. "The Great Stone Face," *Film Quarterly,* XII, 1 (Fall 1958), 10–15. A good short introduction.

Canby, Vincent. "Buster Keaton's Five-Star 'General'," New York *Times,* 1 August 1971, Sec. 2, 1, 18. On the TV showing of the film; a lively little essay.

Coursodon, Jean-Pierre. *Keaton et Cie, les burlesques américains du "muet." Cinéma d'aujourd'hui 25.* Paris: Editions Seghers, 1964. A kind of grab-bag of materials relating to the American silent comedians (excluding Chaplin and Sennett); Coursodon's own essay on BK (pp. 51–63) is the most valuable item in the collection.

Erebe, Judith. "Sur le film comique et singulièrement sur Buster Keaton," *Crapouillot* (août 1927), 26–30. Splendidly provocative, and by far the best piece on BK to have emerged from the 1920s.

Gilliatt, Penelope. "Buster Keaton," *Film 70/71,* ed. David Denby. New York: Simon and Schuster, 1971, 269–76. The starting-point is a visit to BK's house in 1964 that results in a sensitive commentary on BK's work.

Houston, Penelope. Untitled review of *The General, Sight and Sound,* XX, 4 (April–June 1953), 198–99.

———. "The Great Blank Page," *Sight and Sound,* XXXVII, 2 (April 1958), 63–67. Perhaps the best short introduction to BK's work in English.

Kauffman, Stanley. "Buster Keaton Festival," *New Republic* (24 October, 1970), 24, 33. On rediscovering BK.

Kenner, Hugh. Untitled review of Blesh's *Keaton, Film Quarterly,* XX, 1 (Fall 1966), 60–61. Observations on BK by one of our least negligible literary critics.

Lebel, J[ean]-P[atrick]. *Buster Keaton.* Paris: Editions Universitaires, 1964. Trans. P. D. Stovin, London: A. Zwemmer; New York: A. S. Barnes, 1967. By far the most controversial work yet inspired by BK, and not easy to characterize briefly. Serious to the point of grimness and yet almost defiantly unstructured, Lebel's book is nonetheless alive with valuable observations. A very difficult case.

Mardore, Michel. "Le plus bel animal du monde," *Cahiers du Cinéma* 130 (avril 1962), 34–37. A highly-wrought philosophical statement, yet very lively.

Mars, François. "Autopsie du gag I," *Cahiers du Cinéma* 113 (novembre 1960), 22–31; "II," *Cahiers* 116 (février 1961) 28–38; "III," *Cahiers* 117 (mars 1961), 32–40; "IV," *Cahiers* 121 (juillet 1961), 32–40. Incomparably the most elaborate theoretical investigation of the cinematic gag yet attempted; many references to BK.

Martin, André. "Buster Keaton vu de dos," *Cinéma 66* 104 (mars 1966), 9–15. In regard to this and the following entry, anything André Martin says about BK is worth attending very carefully indeed.

―――. "Le Mécano de la pantomime," *Cahiers du Cinéma* 86 (août 1958), 18–30. See item directly above.

Mast, Gerald. *A Short History of the Movies.* New York: Pegasus, 1971. Pages 152–60 provide a detailed comparison of *The Gold Rush* and *The General.*

McCaffrey, Donald W. *Four Great Comedians, Chaplin, Lloyd, Keaton, Langdon.* London: A. Zwemmer; New York: A. S. Barnes, 1968. Keaton is alluded to throughout and discussed in detail on pages 83–104 and 121–27. Carefully researched, but how is one to respond to such assertions as "[Keaton's] little clown was a struggling, dead-panned dunce . . . "?

Robinson, David. *Buster Keaton.* Bloomington: Indiana University Press, 1969. By far the most ambitious critical study of BK in English, with many pages of sympathetic and alert commentary. Essential.

Schmitz, John. "Buster sur le qui-vive," *Cahiers du Cinéma* 58 (août 1958), 11–14. A brief but very sensitive appreciation.

rental sources

Audio Film Center, 34 MacQuestern Parkway South, Mt. Vernon, New York, 10550

Clem Williams Films, 623 Centre Ave., Pittsburgh, Pennsylvania, 15219

Contemporary Films, Princeton Road, Hightstown, New Jersey, 08520

Cooper's Classic Film Rental Service, Northgate Shopping Center, Eaton, Ohio, 45320

Em Gee Film Library, 4931 Gloria Ave., Encino, California, 91316

Minot Films, Minot Building, Milbridge, Maine, 04658

Radim Films, 17 W. 60th St., New York City, New York, 10023

Standard Film Service, 14710 W. Warren Avenue, Dearborn, Michigan, 48126

Swank Motion Pictures, 2151 Marion Place, Baldwin, Long Island, New York, 11510; 2015 South Jefferson Avenue, St. Louis, Missouri, 63166.

purchase sources

Blackhawk Films, Eastin-Phelan Corp., Davenport, Louisiana

Edward Finney, 1578 Queens Road, Hollywood, California, 90069

Entertainment Films, c/o The Film Scene, 1 Beekman Place, New York City, New York, 10038

notes

3. THE DIRECTOR

1. *Keaton* (New York: Macmillan, 1966), 32. I am indebted to Blesh for most of my information about Keaton's early years.

2. Even the experts can't be sure of the precise number: see David Robinson, *Buster Keaton* (Bloomington: Indiana University Press, 1969), 27–28 and 30–31.

3. *Buster Keaton*, 30.

4. Buster Keaton "with" Charles Samuels, *My Wonderful World of Slapstick* (London: George Allen & Unwin, 1969), 93.

5. *Buster Keaton*, 61.

4. THE PRODUCTION

1. Christopher Bishop, "[An Interview With] Buster Keaton." in *Interviews With Film Directors,* ed. Andrew Sarris (New York: Avon Books, 1969), 283.

2. "Comedy's Greatest Era," in *Film: An Anthology,* ed. Daniel Talbot (Berkeley: University of California Press, 1970), 143.

3. "Autopsie du gag II," *Cahiers du Cinéma,* No. 116 (février 1961), 29.

4. See Sarris, *Interviews,* p. 277 and p. 284; Keaton, *My Wonderful World . . .,* p. 129; Arthur B. Friedman, "Keaton: An Interview," *Film Quarterly,* XIX (Summer 1966), 2.

5. *Keaton,* 275–77.

6. *Keaton,* 379–80.

7. The full filmography is in Blesh, *Keaton,* 373–81.

5. ANALYSIS

1. *Buster Keaton,* trans. P. D. Stovin (London: A. Zwemmer, New York: A. S. Barnes, 1967), 25.

2. It's worth noting that the gesture also echoes a famous one by Lillian Gish in Griffith's *Broken Blossoms,* and that the leading female character of *Go West,* who happens to be a cow, bears the name ("Brown Eyes") of the heroine of one section of *Intolerance.* Keaton's apparent distaste for Griffith is further illustrated in *The Three Ages,* the tripartite structure of which is in part a conscious parodic comment on *Intolerance.*

3. *The American Cinema: Directors and Directions* (New York: Dutton, 1969), 51.

4. *Buster Keaton,* 25.

5. *The American Cinema,* 63.

6. *The American Cinema,* 62–63.

7. *Buster Keaton,* 92.

8. Keaton, *World,* 130.

9. "Buster Keaton's Five-Star 'General'," New York *Times,* August 1, 1971, Sec. 2, 18.

10. *Buster Keaton,* 149.

11. Review of *The General, Sight and Sound,* XXII (April–June 1953), 198–99.

6. SUMMARY CRITIQUE

1. Usually falsely attributed to *The Navigator:* see Robinson, *Buster Keaton,* 70.

2. "Notes on Nijinsky Photographs," in *Nijinsky,* ed. Paul Magriel (New York: Henry Holt, 1946), 15.

3. "The Great Blank Page," *Sight and Sound,* XXXVII (April 1968), 65.

4. Idem.

5. Untitled review of Blesh's *Keaton, Film Quarterly,* XX (Fall 1966), 61.

6. Sarris, *Interviews,* 280.

7. Robinson, *Buster Keaton,* 110.

8. Cited in Ian Watt, *The Rise of the Novel* (London: Chatto & Windus, 1957), 133.